Intelligent Web Systems

Motivational Tactics for Web-based Intelligent Tutoring System

Mayori

Contents

MOTIVATION AND LITERATURE REVIEW

In 2012, on the way to an international conference, I picked up the current issue of Traveler magazine on the plane, where Andrew Hankinson, "Holiday 2.0: are we changing the way we travel forever?" In his article, he dissects the prominent role of online booking systems and social media sites in tourism over 4 pages. List the web portals and services that helped you organize your complete vacation, including travel, accommodation, meals, optional programs, and meetings with friends.

He analyzes the phenomenon both from the eyes of journalists and investors, and finally draws several conclusions, with which we have to strongly agree based on our own experience: exploiting the online (e-) commercial opportunities provided by the Internet is inevitable for all market participants and a condition for staying afloat. However, the spectacular web portal, the accommodation offer formulated with careful marketing work, is worthless if the visitor, the person who wants to travel, does not trust the given website. Trust is one of the most valuable currencies of today's Internet life, statistics prove it [19] [20] that social portals, the community, and within that the people who most influence the opinion of the community (opinion-formers, or in the terminology of the Barabás paradigm: network "centers", "decision-makers", "influential users"," influencers", cf. Barabas [21] 2013:144-136 and 280) opinion plays a decisive role in our business decisions, a significant part of those who want to travel trust the opinions of their fellow passengers published on social media rather than those written by, for example, a travel agency.

Another important question of trust arises when dealing with a web portal or an IT system: this is none other than the protection of our personal and financial data. In this case, the stake is no longer a right or wrong business decision, but - sometimes - our entire existence. So, when we hear about data theft, surveillance and eavesdropping every day, don't be surprised if users are extremely distrustful. This kind of mistrust makes the work of the creators of intelligent web systems much more difficult and places a special task on marketing and IT specialists to instill adequate trust and awareness in a particular brand, service, or web portal.

Is the Internet really changing our lives and shopping habits?

Undoubtedly. The number of people using the Internet and searching for information is also constantly increasing. While in 2008 this number was 1.4 billion, in 2014 already 2.9 billion, i.e. more than 40% of the world's population, regularly use the opportunities provided by the Internet [3. figure]. This means that every second, 7 new users hungry for information appear in the Internet world.

The initial and current main objective of my research is to make today's web-based systems more efficient, both on normal computer and mobile platforms. An effective web system is intelligent; provides the user with content tailored to the person (gender, age, occupation, nationality, interests, geography, language preferences) and device (computer, phone, tablet or refrigerator display). It does all of this as quickly as possible, because research proves it: it only takes 3 seconds and 57% of visitors have already left the web content there. Additional statistics support that every second of delay takes millions of dollars out of the pockets of high-traffic web portal owners [22].

In light of this, it is understandable why efficient, fast and user-friendly web systems are of particular importance in the business world.

In accordance with the trends of our time, it can be seen more and more that the Internet will be the primary source of information and news as well as the scene of services and commercial activities. Today's people order products and services on Internet sites, read the daily news on the Internet, and even write blogs, forums, and experience reports since the advent of Web 2.0, and get information about their friends and relatives through social portals.

The concept of Web 2.0 was first [1], but the term was popularized by Tim O'Reilly and Dale Dougherty at the Web 2.0 conference organized in 2005. Today, the term is much more than a marketing term, it is actually a summary name for new technologies [2].

Although Web 2.0 appeared in 2005, Tim Berners-Lee, the father of the web, drew attention as early as 1994 to the need to make the web comprehensible to machines [3], then in 2001 [4] also presented the concept of the semantic web to the general public, which was apostrophized even then as the next step of the web, and today it is increasingly referred to as web 3.0. The reason for the strange time confusion is that the semantic web concept appeared before Web 2.0, but due to its complexity and complexity, we still cannot talk about the age of the semantic web.

Right nowthe World Wide Web is typically made up of documents in HTML format, which documents were written in a descriptive language whose primary purpose is to display information. Due to the nature of HTML, web pages contain a series of descriptive symbols (member and attribute names, etc.), which are meant to display the information they describe ("designated") in a suitable way in browsers. In the first decade after the appearance of the web, the only goal was to display information in a digestible form for users. People read the web pages and interpret them, but at the same time the semantic connections between the text parts are not represented in such a way that computers can understand them.

For this reason, it is worth representing the published information in such a way that it is not only for display purposes, but can also be processed by computer systems.

This is exactly the goal of the semantic web, to develop a Web that speaks to machines, i.e. computers can provide even more help on the Web to exploit and automatically (independent of human intervention) processing of information found.

"The Semantic Web is not a separate Web, but a supplement to it, in which information has a well-defined meaning, thus ensuring even more effective cooperation between people and computers" (Tim Berners-Lee, Hendler, 2001)

New technologies also present new challenges to software developers. The Web
In the age of 2.0, web development is no longer only about displaying information on websites, but rather about creating web applications that enable efficient information sharing, provide a rich user experience, and take advantage of the collective intelligence inherent in the power of the community.

All three pillars of the above list (information sharing, user experience, intelligence) are important, I have conducted research related to each area, and I would like to present the related results in detail in my thesis.

THE INTELLIGENT WEB

Although the Web is a very rich source of information, the collection and organization of data poses an increasingly serious task for the systems that serve users. That is why, as a result of research and development, newer and newer technologies appear, which are meant to serve the visitors of individual websites with appropriate content. The collective name of these latest technologies is the intelligent web.

The term web intelligence (WI) in 2000 [5] debuted, according to Ning Zhong et al., the intelligent web is the collective name for artificial intelligence, knowledge representation, data mining, intelligent agents, intelligent social networks, and the application of the knowledge and results acquired in these fields in a new environment.

In addition, WI encourages information technology and artificial intelligence professionals to solve new problems and challenges. WI technologies revolutionize the previously known techniques and methods of information collection, storage, processing, display and sharing.

Jiming Liu[6] defines four levels for the intelligent web, where the techniques and technologies of information technology and artificial intelligence appear.

*Vagan*interpretation is also similar, according to his research, the term intelligent web is a combination of three technologies, web mining, semantic web and web impersonation technologies [7].

After 2000, working with the intelligent web became very popular in professional circles. In 2002, the Web Intelligence Consortium was founded[2], as well as the IEEE Computer Society Technical Committee on Intelligent Informatics, and every year since then research related to WI technology has been presented at the IEEE/WIC/ACM International Joint Conference on Web Intelligence and Intelligent Agent Technology.

The reason for its popularity is no accident, WI, including web impersonation, is one of the research areas that can provide great tools and economic benefits to the e-business industry. The capabilities of the technology, such as the continuous monitoring, recording, and analysis of users' shopping or browsing habits, give retailers a more effective tool than ever before to target and personalize their products and services for sale as precisely as possible.

One of the best ways to increase the user experience is

web personalization, as we can use it to ensure that each visitor receives their own, personalized version of the same web page. Thanks to the technology, the web servers are able to adapt the website to the customer's needs in real time, thereby ensuring that special, unique user experience, during which the visitor feels that the website is almost reading his mind.

Many researchers have already dealt with the subject of personification, such as AR Simon et al [8] from the point of view of targeted marketing, Ning Zhong et al. from the perspective of the wisdom web [9], Su Ho Ha investigated its impact on customer decisions [10], while Wang and Kobsa [11] has developed a suitable method for it, taking into account the protection of personal data. The basic condition of web personalization is the creation of a user profile of the website visitor, and then, based on these profiles, our recommender system can provide relevant content. The first recommender systems appeared already in the early 90s, typically as an extension of the terminology of collaborative filtering, and as the number of researchers and possible areas of use increased, so did the technology itself.

Today, we list here the cooperation-based [12], content-based [13], knowledge-based [14] and demographic screening [15]. These technologies are combined from time to time in order to increase efficiency, so Burke's hybrid recommender system [16], Melville et al. for Content-Boosted Collaborative Filtering [17], while Sobecki Consensus-based recommender system [18] named his own solution.

At the same time, I personally believe that the concept of the intelligent web today, mobile devices and sensors, or if you like the Internet of Things (IoT)[3]and the Internet of Everything (IoE)[4]in the world is much more than what we understood by the term in the last 10-12 years. Acknowledging the work of the researchers listed above, allow us to have our own definition of the concept of the intelligent web:

It is a network of intelligent web devices that are able to implicitly collect as much information as possible about users, their environment and their own state, and from this aggregated information draw conclusions and make recommendations that are tailored to the users of the system and to the application situation.

For a precise understanding of the above definition and to prove its applicability as a kind of general rule, two examples follow.

Problem 1:
An English tourist in Debrecen searches for a restaurant using his smartphone.

Solution 1:
Our intelligent web system lists restaurants in Debrecen within a 500m radius of the tourist's location in English with a resolution and content detail optimized for the user's mobile phone.
Tools:
In this case, our intelligent web system consists of the following devices: 1. smartphone, 2. GPS satellite, 3. central server computer

Operation:

The smartphone contacts the GPS satellite and retrieves the current coordinates.

The information receivedsends it to the central server computer.

The server computerbased on the provided GPS data, it retrieves the list of restaurants within a 500m radius from the central database.

The server contacts the smartphone, retrieves its type, language settings, and screen resolution.

Based on the information received, it selects the restaurant material in English, optimizes the size of the images and content for the device, and then sends it to the user's mobile device.

Problem 2:

A car and its passengers have an accident, the automatic system built into the vehicle must call for help as soon as possible.

Solution 2:

The intelligent system built into the vehicle calls the nearest central hospital, informs the exact location of the accident, the weather conditions, the number of passengers, the speed of the collision, and the extent of the damage to the vehicle.

Tools:

1. sensors built into vehicles, 2. on-board computer, 3. GPS satellite, 4. central health database (server), 5. hospital call center

Operation:

Built into the vehiclesensors detect that an accident has occurred. The on-board computer retrieves the exact coordinates from the GPS satellite.

It creates an information package about the weather conditions from the continuously recorded data of the external temperature and precipitation measuring sensors.

It determines the number of passengers and their weight from the data of the sensors built into the seats, as well as from the driver's driving style.

It contacts the central health database and, based on the received GPS coordinates, retrieves the telephone numbers of the nearest hospitals.

Based on a specific algorithm, it dials the hospitals and delivers the available information to them both as a voice packet and as a data packet.

PROBLEMS

However, research related to intelligent web systems is almost exclusively aimed at optimizing the algorithms that form the core of the method as much as possible, but at the same time, very little is said about which methods and technologies should be used to collect the data that forms the basis of the processing, and what the final result, the output data, should be used for. form should be served to the user.

Both input and output are of particular importance, because without input data, even the most perfect algorithm is worthless, just as any effective artificial intelligence can work behind a bad, slow web portal, if potential customers and visitors would rather run away from the site than browse it.

You might think that nothing is simpler than collecting data about users, because the Internet is all about this, the billions of data. From the point of view of intelligent systems, on the other hand, data related to users and their behavior are of particular importance, which can be obtained in two ways: either we ask the user to enter the data we request (in the form of forms, questionnaires, product evaluations, for example) - this is the so-called explicit data collection, or our intelligent system collects data in the background without the user's knowledge or interference (browsing path, clicks, visited web pages, purchase history, IP address, language settings, etc.) - this is called implicit data collection.

The two technologies can be combined, but there are problems with both: explicit data collection is difficult, on the one hand, users are distrustful and reluctant to provide data, and on the other hand, they regret the time it takes to fill out forms for our pleasure.

Implicit data collection eliminates the previous problems, and its great advantage is that it allows us to collect a huge amount of data.
data? At all, are we aware of what data and information the IT system behind our computer has collected and stored about us the moment we open a website?

WEB DEVELOPMENT

The development of a web-based system imposes many more tasks on developers than a traditional software development; the life cycle of the system, the course of its development, tracking and maintenance are all different from classical software development. It is therefore understandable that traditional development methodologies are not suitable for web-based systems in many cases, and more precisely, they need to be corrected and supplemented. In his book published in 2000, Powell expressed the essence perfectly:

"Web development combines newspaper publishing with software development, marketing with computer technology, internal communication with external relations, art with technology"[23].

Different technical literature defines the concept of web development (web engineering) in different, but basically similar ways. Based on these, we can say that web development is nothing more than a method for developing and organizing knowledge related to web application development. I mostly agree with what was formulated by Murugesan et al., according to which web development is the systematic application of knowledge related to scientific, engineering and management sciences in order to successfully develop, deploy and maintain web-based systems [24].

Adding that Web engineering covers even more disciplines; as can be seen from Powell's characterization, in addition to computer and IT sciences and engineering, specialists who understand management, art, graphics, and the relationship between man and machine are just as indispensable elements of development as marketing specialists.

CHARACTERISTICS OF WEB-BASED SYSTEMS

In order to understand this, let's review the most

important characteristics of web-based systems and the characteristics that distinguish them from traditional software systems. Several people have formulated these criteria several times [25,26,27,28], below I present a dusted off, rethought, updated grouping of these based on my experience.

HETEROGENEOUS USERS

Web applications are used by a large number of users unknown to the system, up to millions of them, who have different demands on the system and different IT skills. That's why the look and feel of the user interface, with particular regard to accessibility guidelines[5]- and the range of services must correspond to this colorful user community, taking into account the very important fact that in the case of web systems we do not have the opportunity to hold training sessions on the use of the system, as opposed to traditional software, where this process is expected and desired.

Your usersthe prominent role of experience

The look and feel of the user are given a prominent role, a very important segment of web development is art and marketing work. The design of the image, the ergonomics of the user interface, and the precise placement of the content are the tasks of separate creative teams. The web system is the face of a given company, organization, or product to the outside world, and user experience plays a much greater role here than in the case of classic software. If a web system does not work well or users are not satisfied with it, it has much more serious consequences for the owner than in the case of traditional software.

DYNAMIC CONTENT

Today's web systems are dynamic and content (database) based. An important part of the development is the possibility of creating content and ensuring continuous content updating; after the very first armed state, the content is different even an hour later. In the case of larger systems - see eBay or Amazon - this content changes and expands every minute.

CONTINUOUS EVOLUTION

Web applications are constantly evolving. That is why it is impossible to provide a complete system specification at the very beginning of the development process, because the functions and services are constantly changing and expanding, especially after the web system has been activated and put into use. Unlike traditional software,

whichthey undergo revision at pre-planned, well-defined intervals, due to the constant change in requirements and functionality of web applications, this work is continuous; at least as much an organizational and management issue as a technical one.

TIGHT DEADLINES

The development of web applications is always subject to extremely tight deadlines, so the pressure on developers is extremely high. A thorough development plan, which is common in classical software development and extends for a period of even longer than a year, does not work here; time is an extremely important factor.

RAPID TECHNOLOGICAL DEVELOPMENT

Technological development in this area is extremely fast, the application and integration of new standards, tools, languages, as well as errors and compatibility problems of early versions multiply the possibility of error.

HETEROGENEOUS SOFTWARE TECHNOLOGY

In addition to all this, we use a lot of different technologies during web development, classic programming languages, script languages, HTML, CSS and XML files and their combination, databases and query languages, multimedia elements and their management software, complex user interfaces, development and auxiliary software, etc.

HETEROGENEOUS HARDWARE ENVIRONMENT

Technological diversity is not enough, the developed web system runs on many different hardware; different screen size, hardware device, network connection and speed.

ADVANCED SECURITY AND DATA PROTECTION

The network structure resulting from the nature of the Web and the orders of magnitude larger number of unidentified users raise many more security and data protection issues than traditional software.

MODELS OF WEB DEVELOPMENT

It can therefore be seen that web-based systems differ from classic software systems in many ways, and this is also true for the development and design process.

The software development process is complicated and complex, it is necessary to model the individual sub-tasks and the relationships between them in order to have a clear and modular structure on the one hand.

The best known and most widespread is the waterfall model, which first appeared in the literature in Winston W. Royce's 1970 article [29], although it is interesting that the term waterfall itself is not mentioned even once in the writing. In fact, it describes the errors and disadvantages of this kind of development process.

However, the model can be used well if the

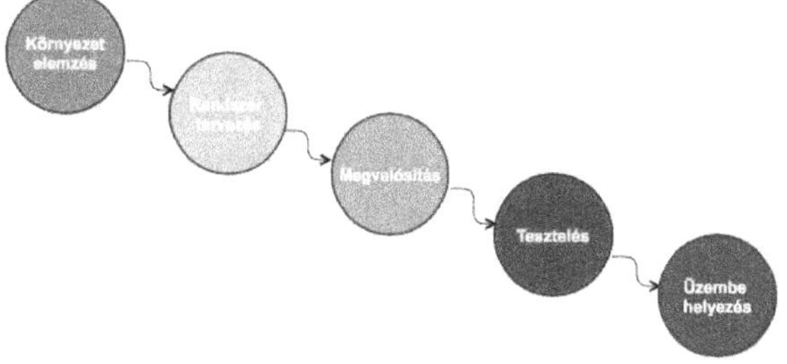

requirements for the system are known at the very beginning of the development. Of course, this requires thorough surveying and research work, not to mention that the customer must also be very well prepared with regard to the expected functionality, because changes during the process are extremely expensive to the extent that after certain steps it is more economical to start the

development from the very beginning.
However, if we have a thorough and detailed plan, everything is to be expected costs and development time can be estimated very well. In addition, the strict development process that fits the plans is less sensitive if we have to part with one of our developers, and due to the precise documentation, the new workforce can be quickly integrated into the team.

The characteristic of the model is that the next phase cannot start until the previous phase has been completed. In this way, a developer or designer delegated to a sub-process can work on another project after finishing his work. In the last phase of the life cycle, the system is handed over to the users, then it becomes clear whether the software fulfills the requirements set out in the original specification or not, and whether the customer got what he wanted.

Unfortunately, in real life, the client cannot define exactly what he wants at the beginning of the project; the requirements change and refine on the fly. That is why the waterfall model is used less and less in business web development, because the waterfall model is not prepared for these changes; once a development phase has been completed, it is almost impossible to make changes to it.

We need a method that is flexible, allows us to regularly consult with the customer on the go, and if a change is needed, make it possible at the lowest cost.

Already in Royce's article, the need for a new, more iterative, more interactive method appears, it is no coincidence that over the years, so many waterfall model alternatives and improved methodologies have been born.

Judge in a separate article [30] describes the characteristics of emerging methodological fashion waves, the latest wave continues even today and has its roots as far back as 1988, Boehm spiral [31] and to Gilb's evolutionary model [32] extend back.

This new trend is agile software development, which in many ways is the opposite of the waterfall model. As soon as a smaller module is ready, the developers hand it over to the user for testing, who can try it out, specify his needs, modify it quickly and efficiently in response to new needs, and then consult with the customer again; continuous consultation and iteration are the basis of agile software development. The method is a guarantee that the user is satisfied and gets what he wanted, even if he was not able to formulate his needs thoroughly enough at the beginning of the development.

A development process similar to the agile method is

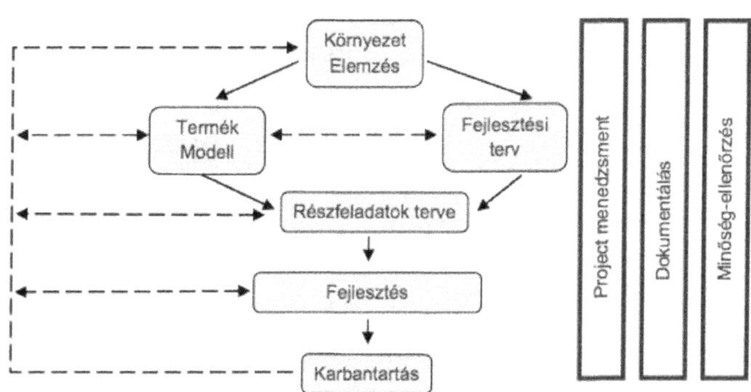

described by Adamkó (5. figure) [33], which belongs to Murugesan (6. figure) [34] process is more modern version and it still stands today. At the same time, in order to meet the demands of today's intelligent and responsive web systems, there is a need for a new, more detailed hybrid method.

JUSTIFICATION OF OWN METHOD

Simply by riding the agile methodology fashion wave, we could say that this is the clear choice for today's development process, but the method has its drawbacks. Continuous consultation is a great tool, but it takes time, and if the customer doesn't get it right, it hinders development. Due to the possibility of constant revision and change, many more specialists (graphics, system designers, front-end, back-end programmers) must be available at the same time, compared to, for example, the waterfall model. In addition to all this, the expected costs and completion date are also difficult to estimate.

It is a reasonable assumption that by combining the advantages of the two systems, we can offer a more efficient method for web development. The consultation with business actors and our own development experience were of great help in the design of the hybrid system, based on which we were able to identify the errors and critical points that may appear during an application development process due to the use of an inappropriate methodology or the neglect of any methodology .

In addition to all this, it is necessary to emphasize again the importance of the user interface, image and design, so the developed hybrid method already includes a development model for this. The previous models have elegantly crossed this point, or just merged it with the system plan, although for the customer and future users - understandably - the look and feel, the so-called "look & feel" is of particular importance.

ADAPTIVE DEVELOPMENT METHOD

USER INTERFACE (UI) DESIGN

TRADITIONAL UI DEVELOPMENT

According to the well-proven business practice so far, a web design is created based on the following process.

After the needs assessment and the analysis of the competitors' websites, the customer explained his ideas about the look, the color scheme, and the functions.

Based on these, a site map, a wireframe, and then 2-3 PhotoShop graphic designs were created.

The customer reviewed these, selected the one that suited him, or asked for modifications, and in the end, an accepted design plan was obtained, which he signed. From this, an HTML template was created, which was then transferred to the software developers (7. figure).

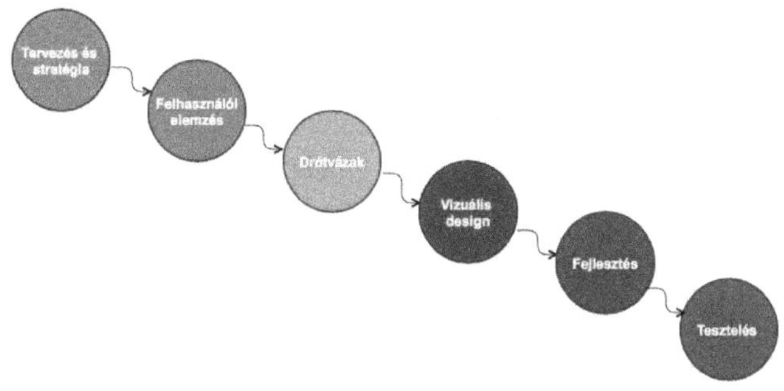

The process is familiar, yes, a classic waterfall model. This process is not viable for adaptive or responsive web systems. It is not possible to create a design plan for each type of device and have it accepted individually by the customer. We should not and should not force this procedure; neither on us nor on the customer. Instead, we use a faster, iterative method.

Viljami [35] and Boulton [36], which provided a starting point for creating the process I developed below.

RESPONSIVE UI DEVELOPMENT

In the age of responsive interfaces, after requirements analysis and information gathering, we implement the following steps.

OUTLINE

After collecting the information, we make a sketch, mostly with paper and pencil, but the Zurb Responsive Sketchsheet is a good service[6] software as well. The sketches are quick, freehand drawings, which are not meant to model the final product, but rather function as a kind of foundation stone in the further design process. Since it can be created extremely quickly, it is a great tool for putting sudden ideas on canvas and showing them to the user. The difference between a sketch and a wireframe is nicely explained in the UXMovement article [37],

WIREFRAME (OPTIONAL)

After the sketch is completed, the wireframe can be created, which is the structure plan of the future interactive user interface. This can already be called a visual model, although many people - especially in the case of small and medium-sized projects - skip this step. Their reasoning is valid, the sketch is fast, the prototype is slow, but interactive and informative. The wireframe is between the two, neither fast nor informative enough for the customer.

PROTOTYPE

At this point, with a combination of HTML and CSS, based on the sketch, a look is created that can be viewed in a browser and, above all, on mobile devices of different types and resolutions. Of course, at this point, basic graphic elements will also appear, but the detailed development will take place in the next step.

DESIGN

Typically, this is the point where the graphic designs are completed using Photoshop, FireWorks, or other graphics software. The elaboration of the details depends on the project, since, like the previous points, this is also an iterative step, as it will be8. shown in fig.

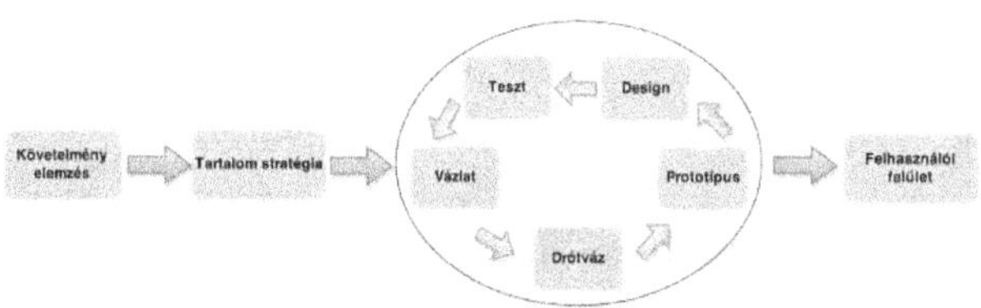

It is clear that the elements of agile software development echo at many points in the development process. Thus, both the user interface and the development process model of our entire web system call for a kind of combined solution.

THE NEW SYSTEM DEVELOPMENT METHOD

No matter how difficult we think the waterfall model

is, it can be used to estimate the expected cost and duration of the project very well. From the point of view of the contract with the customer, these two factors are of prime importance, we must record them at the very beginning of the project. It also doesn't hurt if we manage to collect as much information as possible to prepare the system specification and system plan; a thorough plan will greatly facilitate future work. At the same time, the flexibility of the agile method is essential, in real life the initial functionality expands and changes.

New modules, new menu structure, new look: the competition offers a new service, so let's incorporate it; the marketers came up with a different content arrangement on the fly, let's change it; the dominant

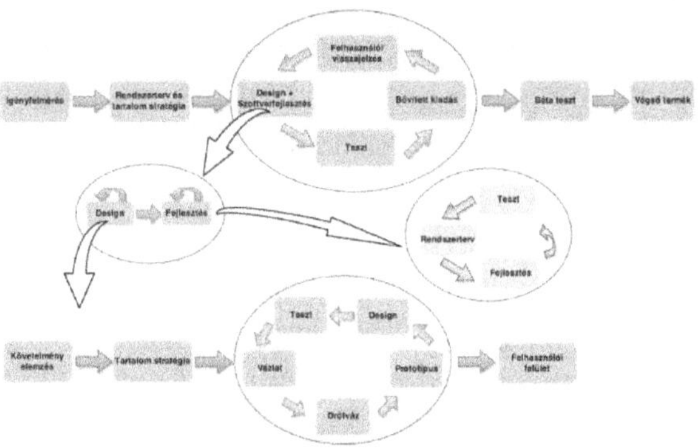

color should not be orange, but light green, a new visual plan should be prepared; still have a geo-sensitive newsletter subscription and associated administration interface. All are examples taken from practice, for which our development process must be prepared.

Based on the above, I created the following process model for the development of today's modern, adaptive web systems.

Let's see what each phase of development entails:

NEEDS ASSESSMENT

The requirements analysis, the needs assessment is the first step of web development, at this point we collect the following information:
We identify those involved in the project and assess their needs and experience. We will get to know the future users of the web system, their possible number of employees, and we will size the system accordingly.
We define the services to be provided by the web system. This step will form the basis of the design of the menu and navigation system, the various modules of the web portal will also be determined based on this information.
We determine what information should be displayed on the website, how this information is accessible and how often this information will change.

We assess the customer's needs in terms of look, appearance, security and operation.
We get to know similar websites,with the web systems of competitors, we study their services, strengths and limitations. This step is particularly useful in collecting the information defined in point 3, the customer can formulate his needs much sooner if he sees concrete samples and ideas.

SYSTEM DESIGN AND CONTENT STRATEGY

When preparing the system plan, we define the system components and the connections between them. Here we describe the network and server connections (be it client-server, web, application or database server), as well as the various modules of the system and the functions and services that each module implements. At this point, the application of a design pattern enters, the system architecture is defined here, the user interface, the data model and the application logic are created here. Due to the agile methodological characteristics, the initial functions and services of the system may change later, but the design pattern relevant to the development, the applicable hardware and software technologies, and frameworks are recorded here.

The content strategy deserves special attention due to its responsiveness; not because you need to provide different content for mobile devices than for desktop computers, in fact! One of the golden rules of responsive development: Mobile users want to see the same content as desktop users. The idea that the mobile view of a web system is a dumbed-down version of a normal web portal is a mistake. Just like if someone thinks of displaying their website designed for a 960 pixel wide user interface one-on-one on a smartphone with a resolution of 320 or 480 pixels.

The correct and justified content strategy is the "mobile-first" trend, i.e., although it is unusual at first and differs from the practice so far, we should prepare our plans for the mobile platform first. The method has two important advantages, one business and the other planning:

INCREASING MOBILE USAGE

Business Insider's November 2013 survey [38], 60%

of online devices are smartphones or tablets, mobile data traffic accounts for 20% of internet traffic, 20% of these users already make their purchases on a mobile device; moreover, all three numbers show a clear, increasing trend.

BETTER THOUGHT OUT CONTENT

The smaller screen size helps us to think more carefully about the order of importance of the information and services to be displayed, the size limitations force us to relegate the less important elements to the background. A clean, to-the-point user interface has greater marketing value, is clear, fast and most importantly: the mobile user is satisfied. At the same time, clean content does not necessarily mean less, but rather much better segmented information, in fact, this design method can be applied not only to mobile platforms, but is also in line with the increasingly general principles of barrier-free and universal design. Of course, more graphic elements, larger images, more detailed diagrams, longer textual descriptions can be placed on a larger screen,

ITERATIVE DESIGN AND SOFTWARE DEVELOPMENT

The steps for developing the user interface were described in the previous chapter, the iterative process used there is part of our complete development process. After the graphic plan for one of the user interfaces is completed, the HTML template is transferred to the front-end and back-end developers together with the system plans. Here we immediately come to a problem that is also current. How to connect existing client-side and server-side frameworks with both a theoretical approach and practical technology. Chapter 6 of our dissertation offers a solution to this.

In any case, software development at this level also follows the agile methodology, a software module is created based on the system plan, followed by a test and further refinement; the process is cyclic (9. figure).

TEST, EXTENDED EDITION, USER FEEDBACK

After the design and program code have been assembled, testing can begin, and then a new, expanded edition can be shown to the user. The customer can immediately test and comment on the system and functionality that has been completed so far, and based on the feedback, another correction and another iteration will follow. It is worth noting that we are talking about a cycle of 1-2 weeks, i.e. the development process is extremely fast. The customer is satisfied, on the one hand, because we constantly ask for his opinion, and on the other hand, because he sees that his dream system is developing rapidly.

BETA TEST, FINAL PRODUCT

After all system elements are in place, beta testing, quality control, minor bug fixes can come, and then the final product can be launched. This step obviously cannot be done in two sentences, but at the same time - as can be seen in the figure - here we have already returned to the sequential waterfall model, so we will refrain from explaining this point due to space limitations.

The coordination and management of the entire work process requires special project management and teamwork, so compared to classic software development methodologies, this method requires significantly more time, energy, and quality.

INTEGRATED DESIGN PATTERN

The development of today's web applications is not possible without a suitable design pattern, because today rich client-side programming tasks must be performed simultaneously with the usual server-side application development. Whether we are talking about client-side or server-side programming work, the volume of work requires the use of design patterns. This is cumulatively true for a complex web application, where client-server development is necessarily inseparable.

At the same time, web application development differs from traditional software development methods in many ways, so we must definitely offer a new method, a new architecture to today's web developers and web system designers.

MVC

For larger projects, the use of design patterns is essential. There are many design patterns, the most popular of these in both desktop and web environments is MVC.

The Model-View-Controller (Model-View-Controller - MVC) design pattern is not a modern invention, Trygve Reenskaug already saw the need to bring the pattern to life in 1979, then still in the Thing-Model-View-Editor structure, a slightly revised version of which They were already implemented in Smalltalk-80 as Model-View-Controller [39]. It appeared with Smalltalk and since then many variations of it have seen the light of day.

The MVC design pattern classifies the objects of an application into three different groups based on their role in the application: model, view, or controller. However, the pattern not only defines the role of the objects in the application, but also how they can communicate with each other.

A specific MVC object group is often called a layer, for example, a group of models is called a model layer.

MVC is a popular design pattern in the development of web applications, and its use has many advantages. The objects of applications equipped with MVC are much more reusable, their interfaces are more precisely defined, and the application itself can be expanded much more easily than other applications.

MODEL

By the Model object, we mean both the data we work on in our application, as well as the definition of the logic and calculation processes that process, modify, and manipulate this data. For example, a model object can represent a character in a computer game or a contact in the phone book. Of course, the model object can be connected to other model objects with one-to-one or one-to-many connections. In a well-designed MVC application, most of the data that is part of the persistent state of our application (this state can be stored either in files or in a database) must be part of the model object even after it has been loaded in our application.

Because model objects represent it for a given problem area

related knowledge and experience, which can then be reused later on for a similar problem or task.

In the standard case, the Model object is not directly related to the View objects. This is an important requirement, because the data and the view are usually very closely related. View objects display data, for example, and the view object allows the user to modify this data in the user interface.

However, the correct process is that view layer user actions,

- which create or modify data - communicate through the controller object and result in the creation or update of the model object. The same is true in the other direction; when a model object changes (for example, data arrives over a network connection), it notifies the controller object, which then updates the corresponding view objects.

VIEW

The view object is therefore an object in our application that users can see. The view object knows how to draw itself and how to respond to user actions. The main task of view objects is to display data from the application's model objects and to allow editing of this data. Despite this - we emphasize again - that in an MVC application the view objects are not directly related to the model objects.

Since we regularly use the same view objects again and again in our various applications, there are plenty of prewritten frameworks, libraries, and classes available to developers.

The View objects find out through the Controller objects that a data in the Model has changed and the content on the user interface needs to be updated, and it also informs the Model through the Controller layer if, for example, the user has typed a name or an email address in a text input field.

CONTROLLER

As we saw previously, the Controller object plays a transfer (and transformation, coordination, synchronization, etc.) role between the model and the view objects. The task of the Controller layer is to transmit changes in the view and model layers in one direction and the other. The Controller can also perform setup and coordination tasks within the application, and you can also manage the life cycle of other objects.

The Controller object interprets the user actions performed on the View object and forwards the new or modified data to the Model layer. When the Model objects change, the Controller object passes the new Model data to the View object, which then displays them.

A big advantage of the MVC architecture is that the same Model and Controller can have several Views, so it can be used especially well in a web environment when we want to display the same content on devices with different resolutions (computer, tablet, mobile phone). Of course, this latest trend is also true in the field of mobile application development, to name just one example, when developing iOS systems, the Xcode development environment by default produces Views sized for iPad and iPhone devices in the form of StoryBoards, while the Model and Controller serving them remain the same .

At the same time, we cannot ignore the fact that the MVC architecture formulated in the original Smalltalk allowed certain communication between the Model and the View (10. figure).

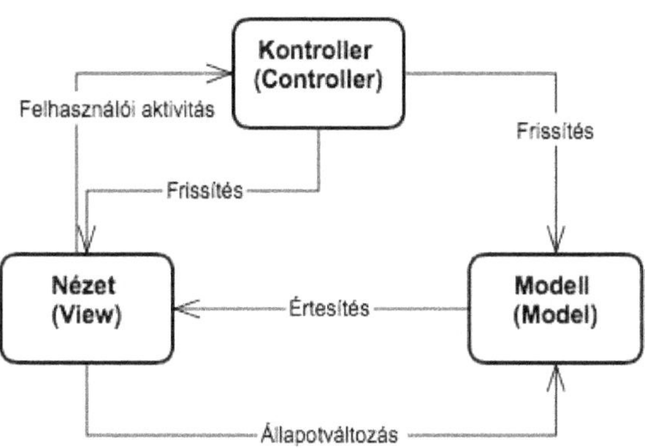

The user performs some action on the View, the View notifies the Controller about this in the form of an event. As a result of the event, the Controller either updates the View or calls the Model to change its state, depending on the logic of our application. The Model changes its state, then notifies the View about the fact, and the View retrieves the changed Model state.

Quite a lot of today's publications describe and use this, the MVC architecture in the traditional sense, which, in truth, fulfills the basic requirements. Because the View does not modify the Model, the Model does not have direct access to the contents of the View, this is the responsibility of the Controller all the way.

THE SHORTCOMINGS OF THE ORIGINAL MVC PATTERN

At the same time, a problem still arises in connection with this design pattern, which mostly affects reusability. In an MVC application, the Model and View objects are the most reusable elements of the application. The user encounters the View objects almost exclusively, for him the View is the application itself. Consistent, predictable and familiar operation is essential, and this requires a high degree of reusability of the elements.

The Model objects clearly unite the data of a given problem area and the processes related to it, here it is even more justified that we can reuse our once written and prepared Models in other applications as well. Taking all of this into account, it is best to handle the Model and View objects independently during the design work, this greatly increases the flexibility of our application and the reuse of components.

Accordingly, the MVC design pattern is a new type used in the Objective-C Cocoa framework [40] version should also be used in our modern web-based developments, because in the age of the responsive, intelligent web, based on the same Model and Controller, there may even be hundreds of Views, or the same View may belong to several different Models.

Citing the first as an example, an intelligent web portal is able

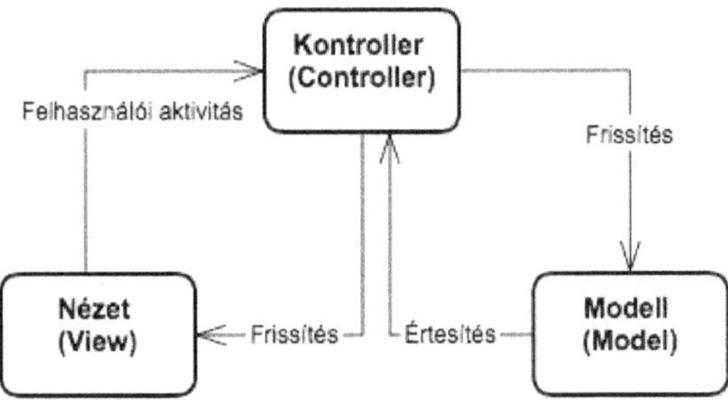

to provide a different user interface for each of its users depending on their device type, individual preferences, and geographic location. While in the second case, it is a web flight ticket booking system written for a smartphone - such is Kayak[7] or SkyScanner[8] - it collects the cheapest and best offers from different, ever-expanding Models - from different online booking systems in the world - for a single View, user interface.

It should be noted that according to the original Smalltalk MVC concept, the primary task of the Controller is to react to user events, i.e. it acts as an intermediary between the user and the application, updating the Model as a functionality by-product. Today, however, the Controller is used in most implementations as a separator separating the View from the Model, which was originally the task of the Observer.

Of course, nearly 35 years have passed since the introduction of MVC, many new, reinterpreted versions of the design pattern have appeared, adapted to today's modern software development needs. Such a modified, somewhat renamed design trend is Model-View-Presenter MVP.

MVP

MVP is a revised version of MVC, but the difference is not easy to define, because there are several different design patterns called MVP.

The original MVP model was formulated in 1996 by Mike Potel, head of technology at Taligent Inc. - later acquired by IBM - under the name Taligent Programming Model, which then became known as MVP due to its structural structure [41].

TALIGENTMVP

Potel used the original Smalltalk MVC pattern as a basis, where, taking a text input field as an example of the GUI elements, the text pre-entered in the field is the Model, the View component receives the data from the Model and determines how that data should be displayed on the screen, for example in the form of a text input field and the text entered into it. The task of the Controller is to determine how user interactions and events affect changes in the data in the Model. Such a user action is changing the text in the text input field, entering new data. The cycle closes when the Model notifies the View of its state change, which has thereby acknowledged that it needs to redraw the user interface.

The Smalltalk programmers designed and used their GUI objects and classes according to the aforementioned MVC abstraction (12.figure).

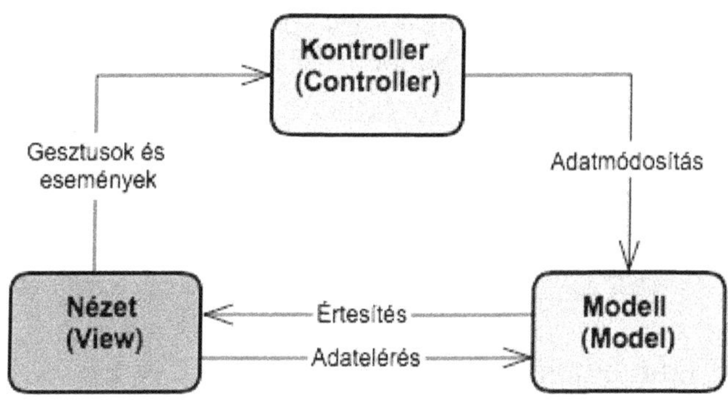

*Potel*its goal was to refine this MVC structure even more, to refine the individual components, discussing them in more detail, thus enabling it to be used successfully during the development of larger, more complex projects.

As a first step, he formally separated the Model, which was handled separately during the development process, from the View-Controller pair (13. figure). He gave the latter the name Presentation, thereby separating data management from the user interface. These are the two main areas that programmers have to deal with, how to handle data and how to display it.

Since data management is a very complex process, the generalization and expansion of the Model component is

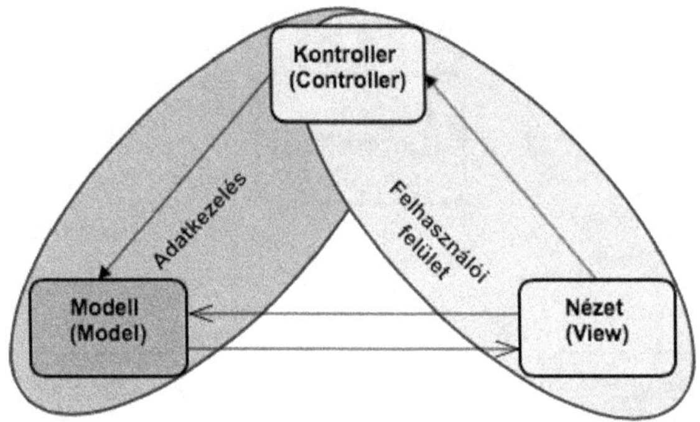

essential in Potel's model (14. figure).

He formulated three main questions, to answer which he created different objects and data management layers within the Model:

- What is data? - This is answered by the Model.
- How do I define the data? - This is answered by the Selections layer.
- How do I change my data? - The Commands layer is suitable for this.

In this case, the Model contains the data itself and the business logic.

The Selections component determines which slice of the data from the Model we want to perform an operation on. The result is a data row, column, or single element that meets the given condition.

Commands determine what operations can be performed on the data. Delete, insert, modify, save, print and more.

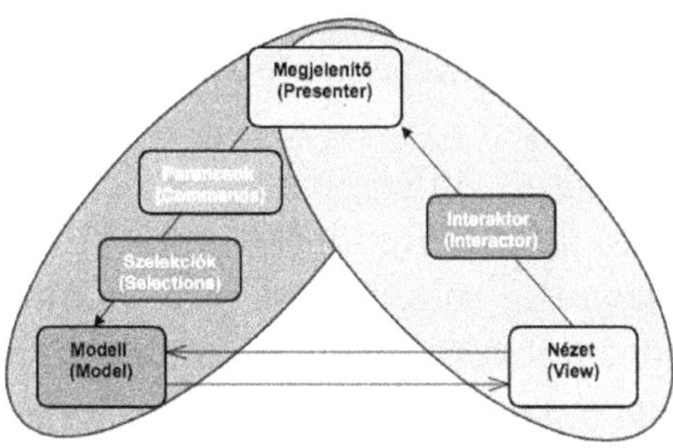

Another major phase of the programming work is the design, operation, and connection of the user interface with the Model. In this way, a few questions are formulated on the user side as well, to which the programmers must provide answers.

How do I display the data? - View
How do user events affect my data? - Interactor
How do I connect the entire system? - Presenter

The View is the visual representation of the Model, we mean the user interface, i.e. the screen, the GUI elements that appear on it.

Interactors are the components that determine how user events can be responded to operations capable of changing data in the Model. An interactor is, for example, a mouse movement, a keystroke, drag&drop or the selection of menu items or checkboxes.

The Presenter summarizes the operation of all

components within the application. It raised the functionality of Smalltalk's Controller to the level of the application layer, its task is to create the appropriate Models, Selections, Commands, Views, Interactors, and manage the application's workflow.

The most obvious difference between Taligent's MVP and MVC lies in the Renderer and Interactors. The Presenter plays the role of a general manager, but the Interactors are not responsible for catching user events, so it is not necessary for each graphic element (widget) in the View to have its own Presenter, as was the case with Smalltalk Controllers. Usually, a Presenter belongs to a given View, in some cases a Presenter can even manage several Views.

Actually, Interactors are similar to Smalltalk-80 Controllers, they are the ones who react to user events and call the appropriate Commands and Selections of the Model [42].

DOLPHIN SMALLTALK MVP

The Dolphin Smalltalk team made the original MVP pattern simpler in the sense that they omitted the Interactor, Command, Selector elements from the architecture definition, and even the Display function became simpler; it has changed from a subsystem management component to a mediator whose task is to update the Model based on information from the View. They noticed that the concept of the MVC Controller, whose primary task was to react to user events, no longer really corresponds to today's development frameworks, where native widgets are already able to handle these events directly.

Of course, we have to note right away that the operation of the GUI elements and widgets - which these frameworks have by default - can easily be represented and mapped to the original MVC architecture, and today's fairly popular client-side JavaScript / Ajax frameworks do exactly that.

Accordingly, in the Dolphin MVP design pattern (15. Fig.) the View is the one that intercepts user-generated events. The View then delegates these events to the Renderer, who then modifies the Model accordingly. Thus, we can notice an important difference between MVC and Dolphin MVP, namely that in this case the primary task of the Presenter is to modify the Model, and catching user events is a kind of by-product, a secondary function, because this task is mainly assigned to the View [43].

MVVM

Finally, we must not forget about MVVM, a design pattern mostly used by Microsoft platform developers (16. figure).

MVVM is Martin Fowler's Presentation Model[44]Its

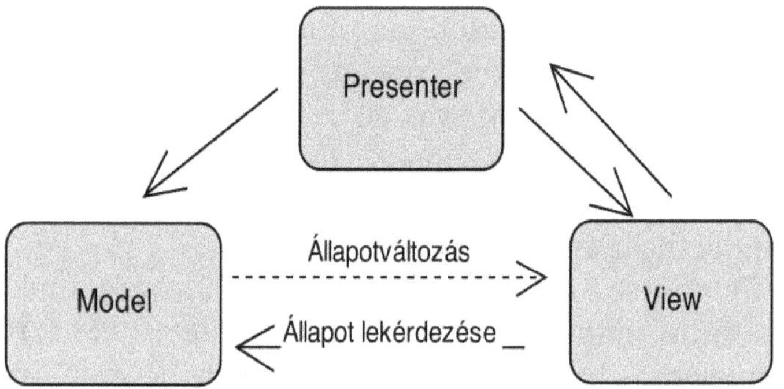

version, implemented by Microsoft, has become popular and known for its use in the Microsoft Presentation Foundation (MPF) and Silverlight frameworks [45].

The main task of MVVM is to separate the user interface from the underlying business logic. With its help, individual components of the application can be tested more simply and developed much more easily independently of each other. The MVVM sample is made up of the following elements:

Model corresponds to the concept of Model used in the MVC architecture.

View, the user interface itself. It displays information for the user and triggers events in response to user interactions.

ViewModel, the bridge between the View and the Model. Each View has its own ViewModel. The ViewModel receives data from the Model and then converts it into a format suitable for the View. It notifies the View if the underlying data has changed, and updates the data in the Model based on events in the user interface [46].

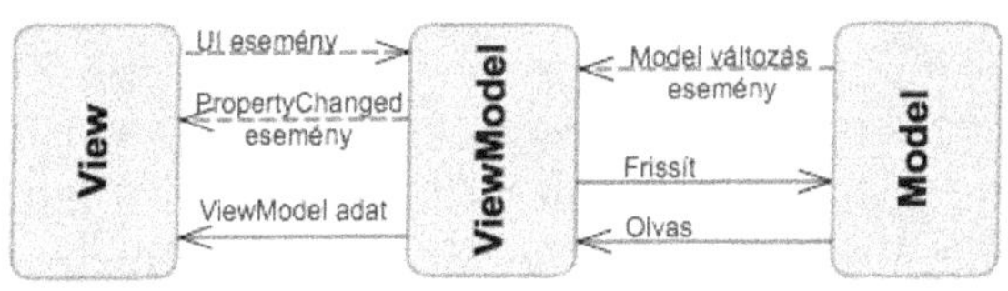

Although the structure is similar to the architecture of MVP in many ways, according to Microsoft's idea, MVP is more suitable for implementing traditional server-generated web pages and the request / response paradigm, while MVVM is a pattern optimized for implementing rich client applications, where the client-side business logic and application state is maintained by interactions between users and services. With the help of the pattern, two-way data bindings can be easily implemented, for example data binding with a declarative approach can be used to connect the View and the View Model, instead of having to write program codes to connect the two. Thus, by connecting the properties of the View to the ViewModel, we do not need to write a single line of code so that the ViewModel updates the View when necessary;

Unlike the MVP's Render element, the ViewModel does not need a reference to the View. It is possible to connect the View and the View Model
means that if the value of a property in the View Model changes, this new value - because of the data binding - is automatically transmitted to the View. When the user clicks a button on the View, a command in the ViewModel runs and performs the requested task. It is the ViewModel, and never the View, who makes changes to the data in the Model.

At the same time, several developers question the correctness of the pattern, or more precisely, the practical application of the pattern. The problem is that many people want to condense the business and application logic into the View Model.

They can't access the View, because it's just a simple user interface. You don't know where the data comes from, you only know how to display it.

The Model contains the data itself, from which the ViewModel is managed, obviously the application logic cannot go there again.

So the View Model remains, which basically contains a subset of the data in the Model, as well as the commands to which the View is bound. Including the application logic, the View Model swells enormously, and error correction and testing become extremely difficult.

That is why it is justified to supplement the MVVM model with a Controller element, which is referred to in the industry as the MVCVM architecture.

The task of the Controller is to implement the application logic and to combine the independent components into a complete application. We have met this functionality before, although it was called by a different name then and there. Indeed, Taligent's MVP Visualizer component performed just this function.

So it can be seen that many people have transformed the MVC architecture in many different ways, according to the needs of the age or their own technology, and even the same design pattern is interpreted in different ways by professionals. Josh Smith describes the situation well [47] apt statement:

"If you sit ten programmers in a room to discuss what the Model-View-Controller design pattern is, you will leave with twelve different opinions at the end of the conversation."

YOUR OWN DESIGN PATTERN

The idea of developing one's own model is a reaction to development needs and experiences from industry and the service sector (e.g. tourism web portals). With the new design architecture, I tried to formalize the ad-hoc type of solutions, and at the same time I immediately offer a practical sample to verify the theoretical research.

THE STARTING SYSTEM

During the presentation of the different design patterns, we noticed that MVP or MVVM systems, different from the classic MVC pattern, tried to replace the Controller in both cases, and then it also became clear that we cannot create a complex application without the Controller function. In any case, we like the original MVC architecture, its slightly modified Cocoa version, in which the View and the Model communicate with each other through the Controller. Our choice is also justified by the fact that MVC frameworks are the most common on both the client and server side. So let's see how these systems are built in practice.

With server-side solutions, developers have more experience, they mostly use this set of tools. The Model-View-Controller trio is illustrated through the following example.

The Model is responsible for maintaining contact with the database, it reads and writes the table data, and the Model contains the PHP classes that we wrote for data management and data structure representation. Such a class can be e.g. a Person whose properties are name, address, email, phone number, while its methods are getNev(), setNev(), etc. Obviously, the methods are properly implemented in order to have, for example, data validation before a database operation.

The Controller's task is to prepare the data from the Model for the View or to request data from the Model based on user interaction on the View. These interactions typically come in the form of HTTP (GET or POST) requests. As we indicated earlier, the application logic is also placed in the Controller module, which is an extension of the concept compared to the classic MVC structure.

Nézet is responsible for generating and displaying the

current HTML content; In a PHP environment, a view is typically a template. The templates are standard HTML and so-called contain template -{tag}- members. These {tag}s can be simple variables, methods, iterations, selections, which the template engine translates into php code, and the result of running (interpreting) the code is included
instead of {tag}s. Although you can safely combine PHP code with HTML tags during native PHP programming, template tags are more transparent, shorter and, ideally, do not depend on the underlying language.

The separation of View and Model is easy to handle using templates, but nowadays, due to the rich content on the client side, working with them is becoming more and more difficult. While previously it was enough to attach a JavaScript library to the template and apply some of its methods, today the sometimes bulky View is burdened with very heavy codes. The work of client-side developers has increased, they use their own set of tools and frameworks, which do not match the service provided by the PHP system.

In addition, client-side and server-side development work can hardly be parallelized with this method, an architecture in which client-side and server-side programmers can work independently would be ideal.

A recommendation would be needed in which the server-side programmer does not have to understand JavaScript, and the client-side developer does not have to understand PHP or the Smarty template.

INTEGRATION OF CLIENT-SERVER MVC

So, the question is how to connect JavaScript MVC with

PHP MVC so that our connected system still conforms to the Model-View-Controller structure.

Approached from the server side, it is clearly the View component that needs further segmentation, because its complexity is what makes the development work difficult. By replacing the View with a complete client-side MVC, our system changes from MVC to M(MVC)C.

If we examine the situation from the client side, the Model component of the MVC architecture is the plain HTML code itself, the View is the CSS file (as many CSS file as many views), while the Controller is the browser itself or the JavaScript program code that extends the capabilities of the browser. In a different approach - especially if there is asynchronous, for example, AJAX-based communication between the client and server - the View is a user interface born from the combination of HTML+CSS+data, the role of the Controller is filled by JavaScript classes and methods, while the Model is nothing else, as data from the web server.

Whichever approach we take, in the client-side approach, the Model is the component through which our system can be adapted to the server-side MVC system.

So it seems a reasonable idea that the client-side MVC considers the data coming from the server side as the data source of its own Model (17. figure), while the server-side system considers serving the client side as the View functionality (18. figure).

For this, according to them, is it necessary to throw out the MVC Model of the client and the MVC View of the server? No, the goal of the solution is to leave the existing frameworks intact, but solve the connection between the two. The bridge, the solution, is a common interface that matches the client-side Model with the server-side View

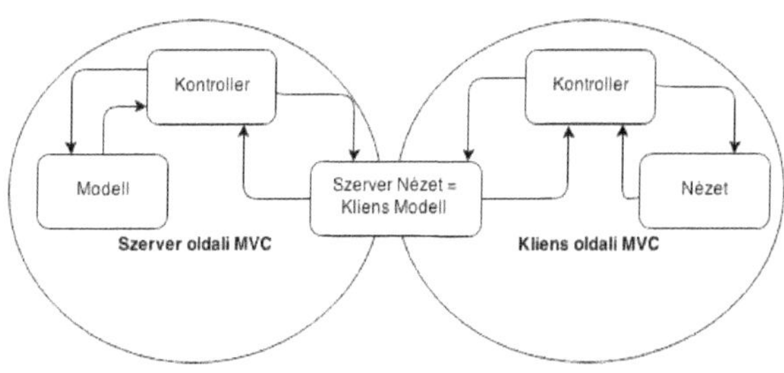

(19. figure).z

The newly created architecture also supports the connection of several different client-side MVC systems to the same PHP system, even if they require data in different formats.

Since the design pattern allows and even supports the matching of several Views to the same system, we can expand the number of Views of the server-side system according to our needs. In this way, we provide the opportunity to provide complete HTML pages in any format that the client-side systems like. Such a typical format is JSON or XML (20. figure).

An important question is whether our new

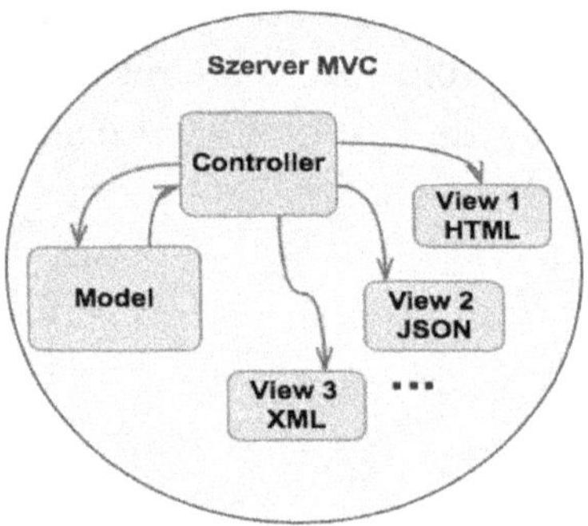

interconnected system still reflects the MVC architecture? Well, no matter which way we approach it, the Cocoa-like structure comes back, practically no changes have taken place from the point of view of the individual systems, only the format of the output (View) and the source of the input (Model) have changed.

THE COMMON INTERFACE

The practical approach requires us to use a short example to illustrate how any JavaScript MVC framework can request data and process the data received from the server. In order to get a complete picture, I will also describe the server-side code of the common interface, the processing of the received request and the sending of the response. The common format in this case will be JSON, for the sake of simplicity we will respond with constant data from the server side and not extracted from a database.

$.ajax() in the functionmethod is responsible for compiling and managing the asynchronous HTTP

request, where type is used to set the request type (GET or POST), url specifies the path of the server-side script receiving the request, data means the data to be sent to the server, dataType is the data returned from the server indicates the type of data, while the true or false value of the cache parameter can be used to specify whether the browser caches the requested page
or not. The successfunction after keyword is executed if the request was successful. In our case, the data coming from the server is displayed in the container element named list, the corresponding HTML source code part looks like below.

The data communication looks as follows (S – Server, K – Client):

The client side compiles an associative array ($_POST) and sends it to the server:

Kmodel → Array([q] => dlist)→SView

In response to which the server returns data in JSON format:

The JSON aboveformat is compiled by the json_encode() PHP function based on the received parameters. In our case, this parameter was the $domain_list associative array.
The new system design model offers a suitable solution for the development of today's modern systems while preserving the traditional MVC paradigms. Another advantage of the created model compared to the previous one is that it can be used to easily integrate

various server and client-side systems.

A NEW MODEL FOR MAKING WEB SYSTEMS FASTER

A significant part of today's web-related research deals with the development of intelligent web systems, and the development of recommendation systems receives special attention and priority. The phenomenon is self-explanatory, since the amount of information available on the web is constantly increasing, in the future only those web services that can provide personalized content to their visitors will be able to survive. The latter finding is more relevant today than ever, but at the same time, experts, Rossi et al., realized this already in 2001
[48] already started dealing with personalized web applications at that time. Since then, many excellent articles have already dealt with content-based [49], cooperation-based [50] or the knowledge base-based [51] recommendations
systems, but today this is not enough.

The rapid spread of mobile devices and the Internet of Things [52] now requires the creation of device-independent, responsive websites.

PROBLEMS

It doesn't matter how brilliant a mathematical model is, how efficient the artificial intelligence behind our web system is, if it can't display adequate information on the website in a unit of time, we lose visitors. The shocking thing is that certain unit of time only 3 seconds.

Research from StrangeLoop Networks and PhoCusWright in 2010 confirms that 57 percent of online customers leave the website after waiting 3 seconds. 80 percent of these customers never return, and more than half of them tell their friends about this negative experience [53].

According to Lohr's article published in the New York Times in 2012 - which is based on research by Google and Microsoft engineers - people visit web pages that are more than 250 milliseconds slower than their competitors much less often [54].

Let's face it, 250 milliseconds isn't much, but based on research, it's still significant if we're talking about a website's sense of speed. Even worse news is that a delay of just 1 second in loading a website results in a 7 percent loss of conversions, 11 percent fewer page views and a 16 percent decrease in customer satisfaction [55]. According to recent research by Econsultancy, global online commerce is losing £1.73 billion in revenue each year due to slow website loading [56].

On top of all that, an average user feels that every website download is 15 percent slower than it actually is. And when they share with others their experience with the speed of the site, they set it as 35 percent slower than it actually was [57].

Speed is therefore a cardinal problem, because every intelligent web service, every recommender system was born to serve eCommerce, increase the number of visitors, increase income and profit. Of course, intelligent web systems play an important role in many other areas of education, research and science, but still, the business world is where the success of our web system is measured in terms of money and milliseconds.

That is why websites must be faster and smarter than ever before, and web developers and performance optimization specialists must reduce the page loading time to less than 3 seconds. Moreover, from 2010, it is now also available to those who want to get higher in Google's search results list, because from this year on, Google PageRank [58] evaluation parameter is the speed of a website [59].

In this part of the thesis, Google Developer [60], Yahoo Yslow [61], as well as Shouders's writings published by O'Reilly [62] [63] I over-applied the optimization techniques used in my own research and development experiences.

I organized, categorized and summarized the currently available and applicable techniques (Appendix - Table 1), and after a series of testing processes, I selected the ones with the best efficiency in terms of increasing the speed of a website.

THEORETICAL BACKGROUND

In order to understand the problem and the solution, we cannot avoid the description of HTTP communication, an in-depth discussion and knowledge of the protocol is necessary so that the applied methods of the research become clear to us.

HTTP REQUEST

HTTP (Hypertext Transfer Protocol) is a World Wide Web Consortium (W3C)[9]and the Internet Engineering Task Force (IETF)[10]transmission protocol for distributed, collaborative, information systems using hypermedia. Since 1990, HTTP has been the general transmission standard of the World Wide Web (WWW), a request-response protocol between client and server.

The first version is HTTP/0.9[11] of course, it is attributed to Tim Berners-Lee, and in 1996, the HTTP/1.0 version was published, now raised to RFC1945 (Request For Comments) level[12]. Currently, the HTTP/1.1 (RFC2616) version is current, which is the corrected edition of RFC2068 '99, originally published in 1997.

The question arises rightly that in the 14 years that have passed since then, there has been no demand for new amendments? Of course. HTTPBIS was established in 2007[13] working group, which on the one hand wants to clarify the currently valid version 1.1, and on the other hand advocates the introduction of HTTP/2.0 that meets the new technological needs.

The fact that he is the leader of the work group shows the importance and significance of the work
Mark Nottingham, formerly of Yahoo!, now a senior designer at Akami; the coordination of the standard is noted by such authors as Mike Belshe, a former development engineer of Google Chrome, and Roberto Peon, an engineer at Google. Joining them as editors are Martin Thomson from Microsoft and Alexey Melnikov from Isode. The discussion document is currently open,

according to the draft version of October 2013, numbered seven, the specialists are waiting for corrections and amendment proposals until April 24, 2014 [64].

Why are the different versions different, why was it necessary to rethink the protocol? The biggest limitation of HTTP/1.0 was that after establishing the TCP connection between the client and the server, only 1 request could go to the server, and then only 1 response could be received; after that the TCP connection was broken. In the case of another request, a new TCP connection, another request-response pair, then disconnection again. This was acceptable for websites of the 'era', but today, when a page contains so many multimedia elements, scripts, and style sheets, it is not a satisfactory solution.

That's why HTTP/1.1 introduced pipelining[14], which in this case means that after the establishment of a TCP connection, several request-responses can be transmitted on the same channel in succession, while the TCP connection is maintained continuously. Thanks to the technology, the client can send new requests to the server without waiting for a response to the previous request, which greatly speeds up communication (21. figure).

At the same time, experts also point out that this development only partially resolved the congestion of requests, because on the one hand, both the server and the client must support this technology - in many browsers, this function is turned off by default [65] - on the other hand, the server must provide the responses in the same order as the incoming requests. Thus, for a connection, the order follows the First-In-First-Out (FIFO) formula. Accordingly, a more robust answer - a

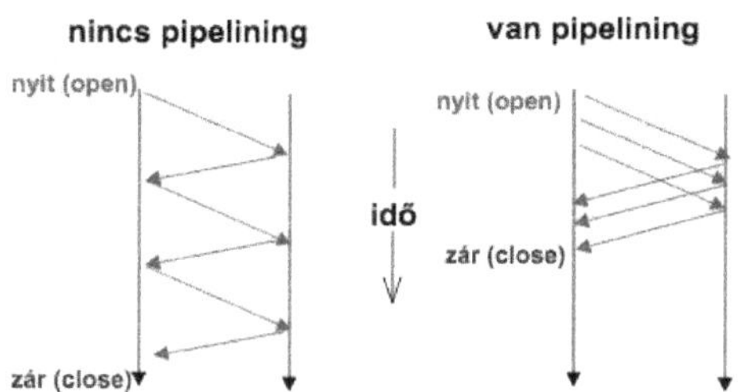

larger image or video - can hold up the traffic behind it for several tens of seconds, which greatly slows down the loading of 1-1 web pages.

HTTP/2.0 is meant to solve this problem, which - among other things - would enable requests to be served according to priority, i.e. by prioritizing the most important requests, performance could be greatly improved. When developing the currently used HTTP/1.1 message format, the primary goal was not to optimize performance, but rather to ensure simple implementation and access. The future 2.0 standard also makes it possible to place independent request-response pairs on the same connection asynchronously, without waiting for responses to requests, and not in FIFO order.

The end result is therefore a much more Internet- and network-friendly protocol, with the use of which significantly fewer concurrent TCP connections must be maintained during client-server communication than before.

After presenting the theoretical introduction and technological background, let's see how HTTP works in practice.
theAccept-Languagelogicallyindicates the preferred language of the response
theAccept-Encodingindicates acceptable encoding of the response - by the client - to the server (in this case, the client can process evengzipwith, evendeflatealso compressed answers with
theConnectionvalue is indicatedthe client tells the server whether it wants to close or maintain the TCP connection after its request has been answered. In this case, thekeep-aliveindicates reservation, otherwise aclosevalue the client would send to the server.
finallytheCache-Controlit is intended to regulate the rapid charging that takes place during communication. THEmax-ageindicates that the client is 'older' than the value specified here as a parameter (in seconds)

refuses to accept an answer. In this case, max-age=0 means that there is no cache, the server must always provide fresh content as a response.

In addition to those listed here, the standard also defines several other HEADER parameters, this information is omitted during the research phase.

After the request goes to the server, a response is received, which also has a standard format, which is as follows:
The first line of the HTTP response is the status line,which also follows a triple format: version - status code - textual justification, each element is separated by 1 space.

Such as the

where the version number is 1.1, the status code is 200, while the justification and explanation is
OK. or the

where the 404 error indicates that the resource requested by the client was not found by the server.

The standard defines 40 different status codes, but allows this code list to be expanded. We classify the status codes into 5 different categories, the first digit of the 3-digit code determines the categories. Accordingly
3xx: Redirection-the further action is required to fulfill the request
need
4xx: Clienterror -a request contains a syntax error or notcan be fulfilled
5xx: Server error-the server cannot fulfill the

otherwise valid request

After the status line - similarly to the structure of requests - the HEADER lines follow.

Date: Sun, 27 Oct 2013 09:20:52 GMT
Server: Apache
X- Powered-By: PHP/5.3.10-1ubuntu3.4 Vary: Accept-Encoding
Content-Encoding: gzip Content-Length: 2788
Keep-Alive: timeout=5, max=100 Connection: Keep-Alive
Content-Type: text/html; charset=UTF-8

the date of the response sent by the server,

theServer, refers to the server software running on the server

theX-Powered-Bya non-standard parameter, it indicates the language and version number of the server-side web application, in our case it is PHP 5.3.10

theCrowfield thenis particularly important when an intermediate server service is wedged between the client and the server, which performs caching, for example. If basically the same content - by which we mean the same resource name - is available in several versions, be it a different language, character encoding, compressed or uncompressed version, we can try to decide on the server side which version is the most suitable for the client. In the decision aCrowfield value helps, in this case it is this valueAccept-Encoding.

THEContent-Encodingfield indicator,how the response is compressed,

theContent-lengthparameter value specifies the size of the body of the response (in bytes)

theKeep-Alivefield of nodesprovides information about the persistent relationship between THEtimeoutparameter indicates in seconds how long the connection will remain in case of idling, while amaxparameter defines the maximum number of simultaneous persistent connections [66].
theConnectionthe sameperforms the same function as in the case of an HTTP request
theContent-typeand specifies the media type and character encoding of the response. In our example, we provided UTF-8 encoded html content to the client.

Under normal circumstances, browser (client) programs do not display this information to the user, and even during the web development workflow, we only dig down to the html source code, but if necessary, there are many tools for an even deeper analysis of HTTP requests and to discover answers.

Perhaps one of the simplest and most popular is the open source Firefox add-on called Firebug[15], at the same time, Chrome HTTP Monitor or WireShark, suitable for many other monitoring functions, are available for those who prefer the Google Chrome

At the same time, the page itself also contains many other resources - images, scripts, style sheets - so the browser must also retrieve these in order to be able to display the web page in its entirety.

The style sheet of the website is retrieved with the following HTTP request-response pair:

The above example shows communication without

cache. At the same time - as we will see in the next chapter - if we turn on the indication of the expiration time of the resources on the server side, it improves the performance of the website. In this case, the response from the server looks like this:

It can be seen that the Expires tag has appeared as a new element, the value of which is a date (in the format defined by RFC 1123). This date indicates to the client how long the given document must be cached, i.e. how long the information provider (the server) considers that the given resource is unchanged, the client does not need to download it again and again, it can store it for the specified time. The rule states that if the value of the Date field specified in the HEADER is equal to or later than the value of the Expires field, the client cannot cache the given resource any further, it must request it from the server again.

Importantto note that ifExpiresand sCache-Control max-agefield is also included in the answer, then amax-ageis overruled by itExpiresvalue specified in .

It is worth drawing attentionalso that the Expires field is not suitable for forcing the client to refresh the browser window or reload the resource. It only has a role in the quick storage mechanism, which consists of checking the expiration status of the given resource before each query.

The question arises as to what content should be included by the client and which content would be a mistake. The own research and development and literature experiences on this topic are fully consistent; The images, multimedia content, style sheets and script files on a website form the group that does not change often, while the html content is the one that is necessary for all

time to download. Why is this so, why can't we cache the html pages?

Nowadays, when we live in the era of dynamic websites, the content of 1-1 serious web portals is updated every minute, but even a simpler company website changes its content every week depending on what new promotions and services it offers its customers. Add to this the fact that the size of the html source code dwarfs the size of an image, sound or video file, and in the case of functions - such as the result of a search, a hit list, a query, a report - which are performed in real time, depending on the user's current preference and the parameters specified by the user, the content of the html page is always different, it would also be a mistake to store an old page, because the content is no longer current.

At the same time, the content of a parlament.jpg uploaded to a website will still contain the same bit combination two days from now; a picture of the Parliament. Of course, during web development, it happens that these contents (image, style sheet, script) are also optimized and modified by the programmers, so during the development period there is no cache, or the cache of the browser is emptied before each page view. As a result, the latest, current content is downloaded from the web server each time. More inexperienced web page creators - forgetting this small but important fact - spend long minutes or hours browsing the source code, saying that everything is fine, but the content is not displayed, and the script they wrote does not run in the browser.

With the knowledge of HTTP communication, we can now start the description of the new method, the first step of which is the creation of the testing environment.

TESTING ENVIRONMENT

In order to properly measure the efficiency of the proposed methods, it is necessary to set up a testing environment in which the speed of the original web page and the optimized web page can be measured using the same methods. There are many free and useful speed measurement systems on the market, Sixrevisions.com has collected the top 20 such tools [67], I selected five of them to measure the research results, by name: a

Among the above, the two defining systems are PageSpeed and Yslow, the others are mostly based on these two systems and on the principles proposed by Google and Yahoo. WebPageTest and Pingdom tend to follow Google's rules, while GTMetrix combines the recommendations of Yslow and PageSpeed. Accordingly, GTMetrix proved to be the most effective analysis system, which, in addition to being able to handle most rules within one system, also has an easy-to-use graphical interface and a detailed statistics creation function.

PREPARATIONS

In order to get a real picture of how the world's most visited web portals are currently doing in terms of speed, I examined the 5 most visited web pages in the following categories:

the first 5 most visited websites in the world,
the top 5 most visited tourist sites in the world, as well as

The top 5 most visited tourist sites in Hungary My choice Alexa's June 2013 ranking[22]based on

*the first-ranked site szallas.hu was replaced due to technical reasons - the analysis tool was not able to analyze it. itthon.hu is a website operated by Magyar Turizmus Zrt.

BelfoldiSzallasok.hu is the sixth examined Hungarian travel portal[23]- which is the 12th among Hungarian travel sites - will be the subject of optimization research.

Summarizing the different categories in a common list, we can notice that the mentioned page in its current state only reaches the modest twelfth place out of sixteen.

OPTIMIZATION

I carried out the optimization activities, following the recommendations of GTMetrix and other methods that proved to be effective during the research. For the sake of comparability, I left the original website unchanged, while I created a subdirectory that provides the optimized content. Below I describe the ten optimization methods that have proven to be the most effective.

OPTIMIZING THE PHYSICAL SIZE OF IMAGES

The images on the web page make up a significant part of the size of a web page, such as the tourist web portal we are examining. That is why it is crucial to pay special attention to optimizing the size of images. The web development experience of the past 12 years, which has only been confirmed by the research work and analysis of the past 5 years, shows that website owners regularly make the mistake of uploading large photos to the web server, which are then adjusted using HTML code on the client side. to size. Although the end result looks the same, it is it slows down page rendering in several ways.

The primary problem is that the full-size image travels over the network from the server to the client. It is now the cheapest digital camera[24]can also
to take 14 megapixel images, which means a resolution of 4000x3000 pixels and a minimum size of 1.3 MB in JPG format[25]. If we upload this image to our website without making any changes, then this one image alone will generate 1.3 MB of data traffic for each of the client machines. At the same time, according to the latest StatCounter data, the average screen resolution is

currently 1366x768 pixels both in Hungary and worldwide [68]. But even if we take the full HD standard resolution as a basis, it is only 1920x1080, i.e. 2.1 megapixels, which is only 368 KB.

The matter is further shaded by the fact that, with the exception of image galleries and image viewers, we rarely place an image large enough to cover the entire screen on a web page. Based on Google's 2010 statistics covering several billion web pages, there are an average of 27.58 images on a web page [69].

Of course, this number also includes the small icons, dividing lines, and holding elements of a few kilobytes; if we take the subject of the research as a basis, this rate is 45%. 18 of the 40 image elements of our web portal belong to this category. Taking Google's statistics as a basis and slightly tipping the scale in favor of thumbnails - let it be 60% -, we can say that an average website contains 11 images that can be significantly reduced in size if resized before uploading to the web server.

Thus, on the client side, the browser does not have to download huge images on the one hand, and on the other hand, it does not have to reduce them to fit the user interface. Of course, under normal conditions, the image width and height parameters specified in the HTML code can even speed up the display of the website.

SPECIFYING THE DIMENSIONS OF IMAGES

Specifying the width and height of images to be displayed in the browser results in faster UI rendering. This is because when the browser displays a web page, it must be able to generate content around repositionable

elements, such as images.
Rendering can start even before the images are downloaded, if we know what to download dimensions of images (width and height).

However, if the dimension value is not specified in the HTML document or the specified values do not match the dimensions of the downloaded image, the browser must redraw the user interface once more after downloading the images. This is unnecessary work and a waste of time, to avoid this we always specify the dimensions of the images either in the <img> tag or using CSS.

APPLICATION OF BROWSER CACHE

Websites are getting richer both graphically and in terms of content, which means that they contain even more scripts, style sheets, images, flash and other media. One might think that, in parallel, the Internet bandwidth is also constantly increasing, so that it is able to serve the new needs as well. This is partially true.

While in 2008 the average bandwidth capacity of an end user in Hungary was 2.5 Mbps, in the first quarter of 2013 this value had more than doubled to 6.6 Mbps. This value is significant even if we only compare it to the first quarter of the previous year, 2012; represents a 12% increase [70].

But at the same time, the number of Internet users also increased. The KSH[26] according to data, in 2012 Hungarian users accounted for 74% of the population [71], this value was only 58.7% in 2008 [72], while in 2010 only 62% [73]. The dynamic development of recent years can be felt, and it can be seen that the increase in bandwidth is a modest consolation; web servers have to serve more users than ever before, albeit with higher bandwidth.

This is why we understand the demand and suggestion that content that has already been downloaded to the client page should not be made to travel through the world wide web again, the browser will store it. As a result, both the size and the number of HTTP requests can be greatly reduced, resulting in faster website loading.

The web server is an Expiresuses a header in the HTTP response to indicate to the client side how long a component can be stored.

If we set the expiration time or the maximum age in the HTTP header part of a static resource, we can instruct the browser that the load previously downloaded resources not from the network, but from the local hard drive. Based on experience, the Expires value should be set to at least 1 month and a maximum of 1 year. Google prefers the Expires member over Cache-Control: max-age , as the former is more widely supported.

Expires headers are mostly used for images, but they are just as effective for scripts, stylesheets and Flash components. We can set the expiration times in the .htaccess file on the server side. Based on the recommendation of GTMetrix, we created a sample that specifies the expiration date for the most frequently used image formats (jpg, png, gif and ico) as well as for style sheets and JavaScripts:

```
<IfModule mod_expires.c> #Enable Expires ExpiresActive
On
#The default directive is ExpiresDefault "access plus 1
```

```
month" #favicon expires
ExpiresByType image/x-icon "access plus 1 year"
#Image expiration time
ExpiresByType image/gif "access plus 1 month"
ExpiresByType image/png "access plus 1 month"
ExpiresByType image/jpg "access plus 1 month"
ExpiresByType image/jpeg "access plus 1 month" #CSS
ExpiresByType text/css "access 1 month" #and finally
JavaScript
ExpiresByType application/javascript "access plus 1
year"
</IfModule>
```

It can be clearly read from the code that 1 month was calculated from the current access time for the images - i.e. when our browser first downloaded the given website -, while for favicon and JavaScript we specified 1 year from the download as the expiration time. As you can see in the first line of the code snippet above, this technique assumes that the mod_expires module is configured on the web server and that our .htaccess file can be processed by the Apache web server.

COMBINING IMAGES USING CSS SPRITES

It is a very good optimization technique to combine our images with the help of CSS sprites into the smallest possible number of files, because the number of HTTP requests, the amount of downloaded data and the time spent on downloading are reduced. A website that contains a lot of images can greatly reduce the download time of the content by concatenating the images into a few files. What does CSS sprite mean?

Basically, it is about using a software to copy the images next to and below each other on a large surface, which after we leave, we process them using CSS on the client side. With the help of CSS, we can position any part of our created single large image, thus always showing the desired part of the image in the right place on the website. We can use several free sprite services, such as CssSprites[27], SpriteMe[28] or SpritePad[29]. SpritePad is a free, beautiful and easy-to-use tool, which we used during the optimization. The images can be easily edited, after assembling them, you can download both the created CSS and the resulting PNG image file.

MINIFY CSS FILES

As a result of reducing the size of CSS files, a smaller file size means faster download, processing and execution. Reducing the size of JavaScript codes has the same result, and there are free tools for both compression methods. Such is YUI Compressor[30] or QTMatrix's own built-in tool.

In practice, minimization means that unnecessary

spaces and line breaks are removed from the code of the style sheet or the script, resulting in a smaller file size. Of course, this later comes at the expense of readability, so if we want to modify our script or style sheet in the future, it is worth keeping the version before the minimization and editing it, or

- in the case of an already minimized style sheet - restore it with a suitable target program.

MERGE AND MINIMIZE EXTERNAL JAVASCRIPT FILES

By combining external (.js) JavaScript files, we can effectively speed up the loading speed of our website, as we can minimize the delay in downloading other resources. Several separate JavaScript files require multiple HTTP requests and always freeze the loading of the website.

Of course, a good web programmer tries to build the website he creates in a modular, reusable way, but while this is an ideal development methodology to follow, we must also take into account that importing modules into the HTML document bit by bit can drastically increase the loading time of the page. First of all, a client who has never visited the given website before - so it has an empty cache - is forced to send a separate HTTP request to obtain each resource, which naturally takes time. Secondly, it is also important to know that most browsers suspend the download of the rest of the website until a JavaScript file has been completely downloaded and processed.

Another useful technique to follow - as we have

already seen in the case of CSS files - is to reduce and minimize the size of JavaScript files.

In the case of a website offering more complex services, developers work with prefabricated plugin collections; supplemented with their own scripts, they can easily reach 2-3 thousand lines. The size of one such file used during the research work was 172 KB, while after minimization it was reduced to 111 KB, i.e. the file size was reduced to 65% of the original size.

Minimization here does not mean physical compression, it's just that unnecessary spaces, paragraphs, and line breaks are removed from nicely structured program code during minimization. Although this makes the new code very difficult for the programmer to read, the smaller file size results in a faster download, and the additional, actual compression process (gzip or deflate) is even more efficient after such an optimization.

There are many free tools for minifying files, so feel free to use JSCompress for this purpose[31], JSMini[32]or the previously mentioned YUI Compressor. Of course, it happens at a later date

we need to modify either our CSS or JavaScript files. It is very difficult to find errors or make changes in the minimized version, so it is worth editing the original, structured structure.

There are two solutions to this; we primarily store the original version before compression, if we need to modify it later, we take it. Secondly, if the original version is no longer available - because we need to make changes to a web portal that has been in operation for several years and may not even have been created by us - then the process of deminimization will help us.

There are also freely available online tools for this, in the course of our work JSBeautifier[33], the ProCSSor[34]and CSS Beautify[35]we used your services.

Google also provides file size recommendations for JavaScript files; above 4096 bytes, it is worth minimizing the scripts.

USE OF A CONTENT DELIVERY NETWORK (CDN).

Yahoo Yslow regularly recommends and recommends the use of a CDN. CDN, i.e. content delivery network, is the summary name of web servers that are designed to provide users with various web content as efficiently as possible. The differentiated geographical location of the servers allows the server closest to the user to provide the content, thus achieving a faster page display. A measure of proximity can be, for example, response time or the number of network nodes. The web server with the fastest response time or the one with the fewest nodes from the client will be the member of the CDN that serves the given user. Content delivery networks are typically paid services, but Techyfuzz [74] recommendation includes five free CDN services.

During the optimization procedure, I tried two of them, but in the end I did not use them. The reason is simple: during the research phase, I tried to use optimization techniques that do not require significant modifications on the server side. At the same time, the use of the CDN also requires the modification of the DNS records of our web domain, which - although it can be done in seconds with the appropriate permissions - is not part of the general client-server work processes.

COMPRESSING COMPONENTS USING GZIP

Compressing resources clearly reduces the amount of data sent over the network. Most modern browsers support the compression of HTML, CSS and JavaScript files, so using the appropriate compression can significantly reduce the download time of certain web content.

To ensure the possibility of compression, we need to configure the web server. gzip or deflate the Content-Encoding header[36] set to mode, you can specify rules for all compressible resources. Again the *.htaccess*file, and we will need to activate the mod_deflate module on our server. Our experience shows that it is definitely worth using the <IfModule mod_deflate.c> directive at the beginning of the compilation of the rules, otherwise we will receive an Internal Server Error error message if the mod_deflate module is inactive.

In the following few lines, we check the existence of the module, and then issue a deflate compression permission for the HTML, CSS and JavaScript files. Of course, for the sake of completeness, we also set the compression for plain text and XML documents.

```
<IfModule mod_deflate.c>
# compression: HTML, JavaScript, CSS, and text and XML
AddOutputFilterByType DEFLATE text/plain
AddOutputFilterByType DEFLATE text/html
AddOutputFilterByType DEFLATE text/xml
```

AddOutputFilterByType DEFLATE text/css AddOutputFilterByType DEFLATE application/xml AddOutputFilterByType DEFLATE application/xhtml+xml AddOutputFilterByType DEFLATE application/rss +xml AddOutputFilterByType DEFLATE application/javascript AddOutputFilterByType DEFLATE application/x-javascript
</IfModule>

The above method is very efficient, but at the same time, the compression and decompression process is time-consuming, so below a certain file size, we lose more time with the compression process than we gain by having a smaller data package travel on the network. Google's experience shows that between 150 and 1000 bytes can be defined as the file size below which compression is no longer worthwhile.

THE RESULT OF OPTIMIZATION

By performing the above optimization tasks, I managed to reduce the number of HTTP requests by 35 percent, while the size of the website was reduced to 32 percent of the original page. An extract of the results of the test performed before and after the modifications can be found in a22. and23. is illustrated in Fig.

As a result of the optimization process, the website not only became the second most optimized website on the Hungarian market, but also rose above the average of the world's leading travel portals. It also overtook sites such as Yahoo and Priceline, moving from 12th to 8th in the overall list (3. spreadsheet).

It is clear that after further fine-tuning, the operation of the website can be made even more efficient, so the research of effective methods and techniques will continue in the future.

RESULT

About to sum it upthe following process should be followed by a software developer in order to make an existing or a newly created web portal fast.

PREPARATIONS BEFORE UPLOADING TO A WEB SERVER

resizing and reducing images
combining images using CSS Sprites
Minify CSS files
Loading CSS files at the beginning of the content
Combining JavaScript files
Minimize JavaScript files
Loading JavaScript files at the end of the content
Specifying the dimensions of images in HTML code

WEB SERVER SETTINGS

- enable compression
- enable flash storage
- creating a subdomain to serve static content

RESPONSIVE, CONTENT-DEPENDENT DISPLAY

RICH INTERNET APPLICATION

In the past couple of years, the development of IT technologies and computer science has been very much oriented towards the web, and the web was quickly apostrophized as the development platform of the future. However, it is no longer clear that the
What does "web as a platform" actually mean?

Basically, the literature discusses three conceptual approaches, the first of which considers web-based user interfaces as a platform, which is based on the basically simple idea of providing users with a web-based interface for existing applications. Instead of creating stand-alone or platform-specific client-server applications.

The second point of view considers the browser itself as the development platform, where the ever-growing toolbox and services of this client-server platform enable the use of new classes and applications, often moving all application logic from the server side to the client side.

According to the third approach, we consider the web-based client-side environment as the development platform; this approach is often called Rich Internet Application (RIA) [75].

We can see many attempts to define Rich Internet Application (RIA) as a concept in the literature, the demand for technology and thus the concept was born around Macromedia in 2002 [76], since then many authors and researchers have dealt with the topic, just to mention a few:
In 2006, Bozzon et al. wrote the following [77] :

"RIAs are versions of web-based systems that provide sophisticated user interfaces for representing complex processes and data, minimize data traffic between the client and server, and the interaction and display layer

transferred from the server to the client side. The RIA is typically loaded by the client, along with some initialization data; then it manages data display and event processing and communicates with the server as soon as the user asks for more information or when it needs to send data to them."

Then in 2008, Santiago Meliá and his colleagues [78], and Paul and Harvey Deitel
[79] formulated the following:

"The user interfaces of web applications traditionally have limited possibilities in terms of usability and interactivity. In order to overcome these limitations, a new type of web applications appeared - their name is Rich Internet Application (RIA) - which offer much richer and more efficient graphical components similar to desktop applications."

RIAs are web applications that provide responsiveness, "rich" services and functionality similar to desktop applications. Early Internet applications supported only simple HTML graphical user interfaces (GUIs). Since these were only capable of serving basic functions, they didn't offer anywhere near the look and feel of desktop applications. RIAs are the results of today's much more advanced technologies, which enable greater responsiveness and the creation of more advanced GUIs."

Finally, in their 2009 Technical Report, Busch and Koch summarized the essence of RIA as follows [80]:

"RIAs are web applications that use data that can be processed both on the client and server side. In addition, the data exchange takes place asynchronously, the client remains responsive while constantly recalculating and updating certain parts of the user interface. "

From all three characterizations, it is clear that "richness", that is, what distinguishes early web applications from today's applications, means a sophisticated, convenient and versatile user interface similar to desktop applications. Continuous responsiveness, i.e. the ability to react immediately to user intervention, is ensured by asynchronous client-server communication. The engine and soul of this is none other than AJAX, which ensures the possibility of minimal, only the most necessary data moving through the communication channel, all in the background, so the GUI can react to the user's intervention and needs at any time.

I have already mentioned the acronym AJAX several times, and it will come up many times in the future, it is time to explain what it is all about.

THE AJAX

AJAX - Asynchronous JavaScript And XML - is not a new technology, but a combination of several different web technologies that can also be used independently. The acronym first appeared in Garett's 2005 article [81], the definition just now also comes from his pen.

The technology itself, according to which the server-side application can exchange data with the client without reloading the website, existed already in 2002 under the name remote scripting [82], but it became really popular when Google engineers started using it; think here of Google Suggest, Gmail or Google Maps services. Although AJAX is a collection of many existing technologies, from the technology package originally described and proposed [83] it is sufficient to use only 3 components. We need

XMLHttpRequest[37] object for asynchronous data communication between client and server - this is the essence of AJAX
I GIVE[38] (Document Object Model) to ensure dynamic display and structure change
and JavaScript for client-side data processing, data display, and integration of previous technologies

The essence of the technology is that AJAX can use the XMLHttpRequest JavaScript object to exchange data with the web server without reloading the given web page. Ajax performs asynchronous data exchange between the browser and the web server (with the help of HTTP requests), thus achieving the fact that instead of downloading the entire web page, it only updates

SYNCHRONOUS COMMUNICATION

To understand the significance of this, we need to examine the client-server communication of the classic web application. Communication - based on a real-life example - looks like this:

1. On the client side, the user browses your website, fills out a form, and then presses a button or clicks on a link. At
Your browser makes http requestssends information to the web server.
The web serverworks, (retrieves data, calculates, authenticates, etc.) then
returns a new HTML page to the client, i.e. the browser (24. figure).

Source: http://www.openajax.org/whitepapers/

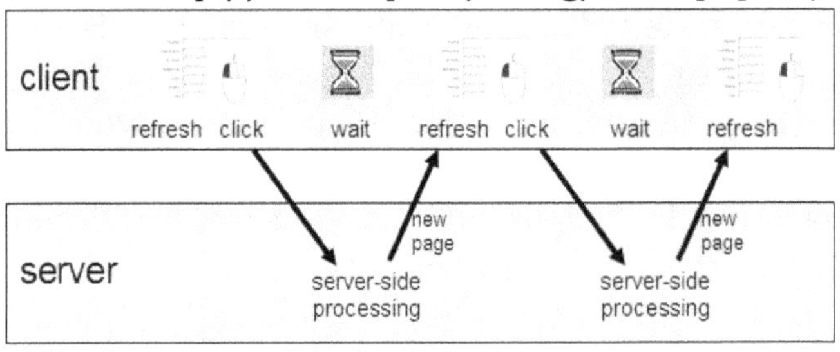

What's wrong with that?

The page stops working until the request to the web server is completed. The user just sits and waits for the answer, the new web page or the result to appear.
The entire page is downloaded (images, scripts, style sheet, HTML elements) despite the fact that - compared to the previous one - only a fraction of it has changed.
As a result, redundant and unnecessary data traffic is generated, the main consequence of which is that we make the user wait even longer.

And this is unacceptable in today's world, as time is one of the most important factors influencing our online shopping decisions.

ASYNCHRONOUS COMMUNICATION

This is where AJAX and the asynchronous communication it carries in its name come into play. In this case, asynchrony refers to the fact that the display of the current page and the background communication with the server are independent of each other. Although the client-server architecture is the same in both cases, there is one very important difference between the two technologies. On the client side sits the Ajax engine, which manages the necessary data exchange between the web server and the web browser. The key word in this case is 'necessary', as occasionally only a small slice

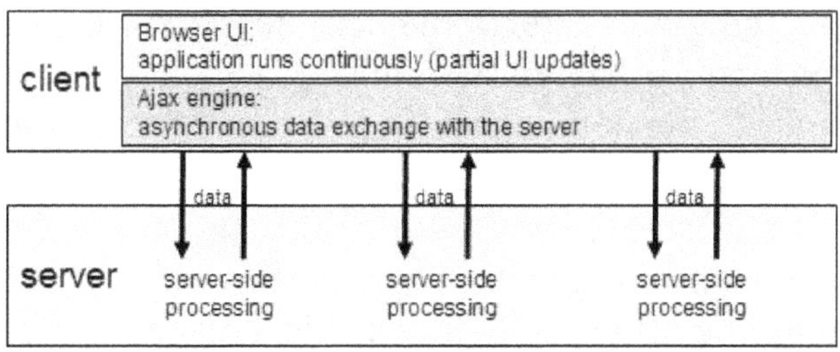

of the entire web page travels through the communication channel and that only when necessary (25. figure).

While AJAX waits in the background for the data to arrive

from the server, the user can use the current page. As soon as the data is received, the AJAX engine displays the new content on the web page without modifying the entire page, but only those parts of it that have been updated or changed.

Because the data of the entire page does not move between the browser and the web server, but only the changed data, communication and the display of new information are much faster.

In addition, it does all this without the usual "flashing when updating" (flickering / blinking), so the user probably doesn't even notice,

that the website he opened already contains new data.

STRUCTURE OF THE AJAX ENGINE

After the general technological description, let's see how such an AJAX engine is built.

Thanks to the popularity of AJAX, many pre-made code libraries can now be found on the Internet, but in this thesis I still created my own AJAX engine. On the one hand, I also use it in other parts of the research, refer to it, and on the other hand, if possible, I prefer to describe its operation through a personal development. Based on this train of thought, the own AJAX engine follows.

The first step is to create an instance of XMLHttpRequest with the following JavaScript statement.

YouAs always, we are now paying close attention to browser compatibility. Internet Explorer names this object differently than Mozilla-based systems, so our function below will be able to create an XMLHttpRequest instance:

As a second step, we have to wait for the response sent by the web server. The onreadystatechange attribute of the XMLHttpRequest object is used for this, and the function assigned to it is executed when the data has arrived at the client.

Our function above will contain the request made in the third step. For this, we will use the methods and attributes of the previously initialized XMLHttpRequest object.

ATTRIBUTES

readyState: indicates the status of the retrieval process and can take 4 different values: 0 – the retrieval has not yet started, 1 – the connection has been established, 2 – the retrieval has been sent, 3
– processing. 4 – done

responseText: the text received from the server, essentially the relevant data we are waiting for

For us, the thing is interesting when the new data has already arrived, i.e. the retrieval process is complete, ready, so we need the following code:

The code snippet above displays the value returned by the web server in the DOM element with the content ID - which is typically a <p> or even more so a <div>. The returned value is contained in the responseText, which is an attribute of the object named http_req, where the http_req object is an instance of XMLHttpRequest.

METHODS

open (mode, url, boolean)
This is the method that opens a communication channel to the web server, with the following parameters:

- *mode*- the method of data transfer, it can be GET or POST, just like in the case of HTML forms
- *url*– the path of the file on the web server that will process the requests of the client side
- *boolean*– can be true or false, this switch indicates whether we want to connect to the web server synchronously or asynchronously. Of course, we will connect asynchronously, because this is the essence of Ajax.

send (string)
We can use the send method to send our request to the open method url
parameter of the program.

The methods usedthey form the following code snippet:

With the open method, we opened the asynchronous communication to the program specified in the url parameter, then for the sake of standard communication - as shown in the example above - we also set the header part of the HTTP request with the setRequestHeader method. After that, the client sent the data specified in the data variable to the web server using the send method.

So let's take a look at what our AJAX engine looks like.

At the end of the program code, there is also a function called UrlapKuld, which is responsible for compiling the data package to be sent to the web server and calling the AjaxMotor function.

THE BUILDING BLOCKS OF THE DEVELOPMENT ENVIRONMENT

The question rightly arises as to whether we will receive any help, toolkit, or guidance for the development of web systems that meet today's expectations and provide a rich user experience?

Although he praises the work of graphic specialists independent of programming work for the spectacular and beautiful graphic elements, the many JavaScript frameworks are responsible for the interactive and increasingly impressive functionality of the components displayed on the GUI, without which no more complex web project can be created today.

It is worth noting that the research so far, as well as the appearance of the RIA, are exclusively about the so-called plugins built into the browser[39] with the help of which he saw the realization of a rich user experience. Thus, Java Applet, JavaFX, Adobe Flash, Flex or Microsoft Silverlight tool system were used, modeled and researched. At the same time, due to the strong expansion of the mobile platform, where these plugins cannot or only be used in a limited way, as well as the fact that the plugins are not necessarily installed on the user's computer, the latest analyzes created several RIA categories, such as there are script-based, plugin-based, and web-based desktop applications.

The difference between a plugin-based web application and a web-based desktop application is not always clear, it is enough to think of an application made with Silverlight, which can be run in a browser as well as independently.

In addition, as indicated in the previous paragraph, plugin-based systems are highly platform-dependent and in some cases do not work at all. That is why, based on our own business experience and the latest trends, we deal with and discuss plugin-free, script-based systems. The foundations of these systems are clearly JavaScript (Ajax) frameworks.

CLIENT-SIDE FRAMEWORKS

The use of open source JavaScript frameworks is an increasingly popular trend in web application development, based on W3Techs.com's analysis of the 10 million most visited websites in January 2014, we can say that 61.8% of today's websites use some kind of
*A given web portal can use several frameworks

It is no coincidence that large companies such as Microsoft, Amazon, The Guardian or Fox News [85] during the development work of recent years, we also chose this framework as the development tool. Strictly speaking, jQuery is not a framework, but rather an integrable script library from which we can build any MVC architecture ourselves. If you still want to use an MVC framework, TodoMVC will help you make the decision[40], where we can choose the framework we like from a very wide range.

SERVER-SIDE FRAMEWORKS

On the server side, the use of framework systems is

perhaps even more widespread, we can find many very popular and easy-to-use systems. The web developer's job is not easy, if he has to choose, the server-side programming language can narrow the circle; we were curious about the most popular languages.

Statistics from W3Trends.com for January 2014 [86], we can say that by far the PHP language is the most popular (26.

The truth is that there are many PHP-based CMS systems (Drupal, Joomla, WordPress, etc.) whose use imposes significantly fewer programming tasks on web developers than using the pure language or development framework. This distorts the picture, it would be worthwhile to learn about the distribution of languages without these systems.

Fortunately, we also get statistics on the use of CMS systems [87]: today 35.2% of websites use some kind of CMS. Assuming that all of these systems are PHP-based, actual PHP usage today is 46.4%, so it is still by far the most popular server-side programming language.

Based on these, we collected PHP-based MVC frameworks. Every developer and professional portal has its own top 10 best frameworks, we list the open source frameworks we consider to be the most popular without claiming to be exhaustive. (CodeIgniter[41], CakePHP[42],Y i i[43], With Lara[44],Symphony[45], Zend Framework[46]).

In a production environment, it seems to be an ideal combination to choose a jQuery-based JavaScript MVC framework on the client side, while on the server side one of the listed 6 PHP systems.

Fortunately, the integrated MVC model is not

language-dependent, so whatever language we choose, the design pattern presented earlier can be applied to it.

Well, once the development environment has been built on both the client and server side, we can start working.

RESPONSIVE OR ADAPTIVE?

Right at the very beginning, we need to clarify the difference between responsive and adaptive display.

Although both methods aim toweb systems should provide the same user experience on different mobile devices and screen sizes, according to the responsive approach, the user interface can be 'fluid' in real time; CSS media queries are used to determine the current size and orientation of the screen on the client side, and then the appearance is transformed based on this. In the case of adaptive display, we prepare the user interfaces in advance for the most typical screen sizes (360, 480, 720, 960 pixel width) and the server provides the current one that matches the resolution of the mobile device.

Opponents of the responsive approach consider the adaptive solution to be faster and more efficient, because in the adaptive case, we only send the client a View made for the current device type or device category.

At the same time, it is against the adaptive solution that it is made for fixed screen sizes, it does not have the flexibility that the responsive interface offers.

However, Google prefers the responsive approach, where the server sends the same HTML code to all devices, and then CSS adjusts the appearance to the appropriate size on the client side [88].

My own terminology differs from this, by adaptivity I mean not only the display depending on the screen size and device, but adaptation related to other needs and characteristics of the user. Be it the language setting, geographical location or even the time of day or season. According to my understanding, responsiveness is only a subset of adaptivity, and I am clearly referring to device-dependent user interface display. The other parameters, which do not apply to the appearance, but to the display

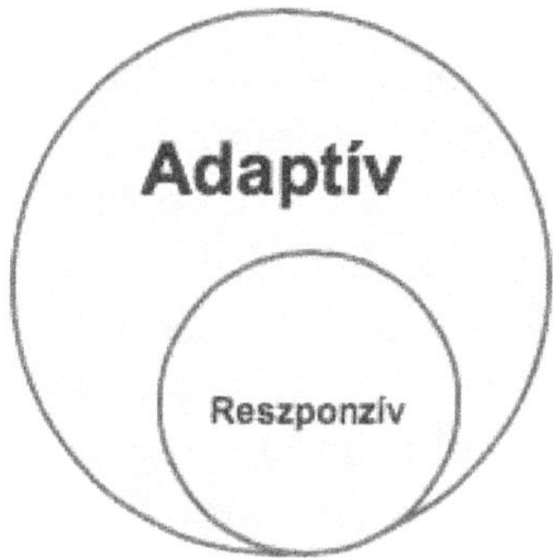

of content, belong to the larger, adaptive set (27. figure).

We must not forget that today our web system appears on smartphones and tablets in the same way as it does on the console screen of our car, the interface of our SmartTV or the display of our refrigerator.

IMPLICIT DATA COLLECTION

The essence of implicit data collection is that we can collect information about the user and his device without disturbing him. We can do this on both the client and server side, both have their advantages and disadvantages. I tried to exploit the advantages of both techniques, so I used a combined method.

CLIENT-SIDE DETECTION

Since our device is the client itself, it seems obvious to get the relevant information from the browser side. It is therefore necessary to detect the type of our device on the one hand, and its services on the other.

Modernizr can be a suitable tool for detecting services[47] using a framework, we can collect valuable information based on JavaScript, while the HTTP header will clearly help us to identify the device.

My undisclosed goal is to store and later analyze user data, so I also send information obtained on the client side to the server, using the same method that I have already described for the Integrated MVC architecture.

SERVER-SIDE DETECTION

On the server side, we can only rely on information from the browser, the most practical element in this regard is the User-Agent header element. A typical User-Agent header from a Macintosh computer running Mac OS X 10.9.1, viewed with Safari 7.0.1, looks like this:

Mozilla/5.0 (Macintosh; Intel Mac OS X 10_9_1) AppleWebKit/537.73.11 (KHTML, like Gecko) Version/7.0.1 Safari/537.73.11

The same with the Firefox browser:
Mozilla/5.0 (Macintosh; Intel Mac OS X 10.9; rv:26.0) Gecko/20100101 Firefox/26.0

Equipped with iOS 7.0.4 operating system - viewed from an iPhone:

Mozilla/5.0 (iPhone; CPU iPhone OS 7_0_4 like Mac OS X) AppleWebKit/537.51.1 (KHTML, like Gecko) Version/7.0 Mobile/11B554a Safari/9537.53

While with a Samsung Galaxy SIII, from the Google Chrome browser:

Mozilla/5.0 (Linux; Android 4.3; GT-I9300 Build/JSS15J) AppleWebKit/537.36 (KHTML, like Gecko) Chrome/31.0.1650.59 Mobile Safari/537.36

To interpret the User-Agent (UA) stringwe can write code ourselves or use business solutions like WURFL[48] or DeviceAtlas[49] projects that maintain an up-to-date database of possible UA combinations and device types.

THE OWN INFORMATION GATHERING MODEL

I have divided the information obtained about the user into 3 different groups based on their main characteristics, and I characterize each group as follows:

DEVICE DETECTION

This typically includes information about the user's hardware device, such as device type, category, browser version, operating system, screen resolution, and installed plugins and fonts.

ENVIRONMENT DETECTION

Under environment, we do not strictly want to map the user's hardware, but rather his real life space. Valuable information is what language you speak, what country and city you live in, who is your Internet Service Provider, what is the speed of your Internet connection, or what is the current date accurate to the millisecond according to your time zone.

BEHAVIOR DETECTION

Behavior detection collects the user's visiting and shopping habits. It's worth finding out when and at what intervals you visit the web portal, what pages you look at, what services you order or don't order at all!

For example, what conclusion can we draw from the fact that if

it's night time AND your device type is a touch screen interface for a car.

The easiest thing to do is to change the style sheet of our web system to a different color scheme that is clearly visible even in the dark.

We can formulate more complex conditions if, for example, a news portal has the sensors we created:

work of the University of Debrecen AND reads medical articles AND in Portuguese AND on weekdays AND between 8am and 6pm

It is quite likely that it is a Portuguese medical student or

visiting medical lecturer.
Again, I need to point out that this information is collected implicitly, i.e. without the user's knowledge or

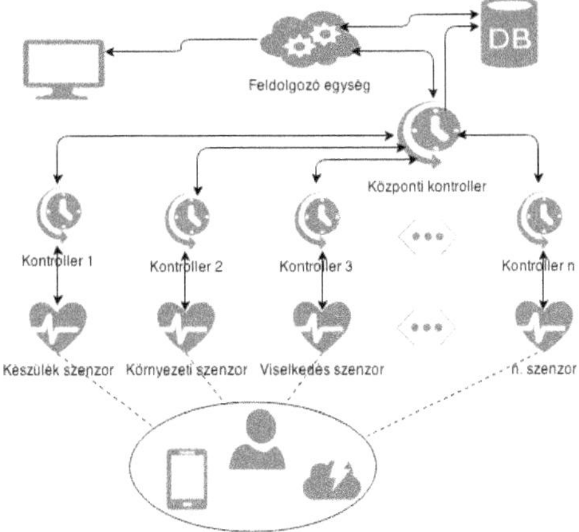

permission, unnoticed by the system, with all its advantages and disadvantages.

I created three sensors to detect properties in the three main categories. I prepared each sensor to detect some typical information, these are summarized in the table below.

The capabilities of the sensors can be improved, thanks to the modular structure they can be expanded at will, and they can be taught to detect new information. True to the practical approach, I also present 4 typical properties, as follows:

IP DECODING - ENVIRONMENTAL SENSOR

Based on the IP address, we can find out a lot of useful

information about the user, among other things, we can decipher their geographic location and the name of their Internet service provider. The client's IP is contained in the server variable $_SERVER['REMOTE_ADDR'], other related information can be queried through various protocols based on central databases.
The free IP API[50]I used your service, which is also free

From Ip2Location Lite[51]more preciseand provides more detailed information. Below I describe the class created for decoding the IP address and the result of the decoding.

The IPDecode class

When deciphering IP addresses, we must take care that the detection is not always accurate. There are service providers with whom - no matter where you are in the country
– the Budapest headquarters appears as a location. To illustrate this, we collected the following information from the same mobile device that produced the result shown in the previous table with a WiFi connection, with a 3G connection.

LANGUAGE DETECTION - ENVIRONMENTAL SENSOR

The language setting of the client can be easily determined from the Accept-Language HTTP header. If we want to answer this in text, I will describe a short class as a solution.

DEVICE DETECTION - DEVICE SENSOR

For the detection, I used the WURFL Cloud service, for which we need to generate a unique API key after registration. A maximum of five features can be requested for the free package, which can of course be freely varied. The complete parameter list containing almost 500

The WURFL CloudUsing a client
After that, with a simple method call

the type and brand of the phone can be queried, or the information whether it is a mobile device (is_smartphone) or a tablet (is_tablet) e.

By viewing the page containing the above code from the previously mentioned Samsung Galaxy S III phone, the following data can be obtained.

We can also use our own implementation to extract operating system and browser data, the User-Agent carries this information. PHP also has a separate method for querying, this is get_browser(), the return value of which is an associative array with the appropriate data.

VISITED WEBSITE DETECTION - BEHAVIOR SENSOR

The server page of the visited website contains the value of the REQUEST_URI key of the $_SERVER array, the exact time of the visit is carried by the REQUEST_TIME value of the same array. The following class shows an example of this:
VisitedPageDetectclass

RESPONSIVE DISPLAY

Once all the information is at our disposal, we have the opportunity to provide optimized content for the user's device in response to the detected properties. The latest method to achieve this is the exploitation of the services provided by CSS, the use of media queries.

The HTML4 and CSS2 versions already supported media-dependent style sheets, so, for example, the same document can have different style sheets if it is displayed on the screen, in print or on TV.
The syntax is as follows:

The current possible parameters are:'all','braille', 'embossed', 'handheld', 'print','projection', 'screen', 'speech', 'tty', 'tv', while new HTML versions may introduce new media types such as'3d-glasses'.

Media queries supplement this syntax with additional expressions that are suitable for returning a true or false value about the existence of a given media property.
the same within a CSS style sheet:

The two rules are the samemeans: if the display takes place on the screen AND its width is at least 600 pixels, then the style definitions in the normal.css style sheet must be applied, or - if the second example is applied - the style definitions between {}.

The standard describes in detail the possible media services [89], supports optimization for mobile devices very well; it can even monitor whether the mobile device is used in portrait or landscape mode.

Meaning: The style definitions must be implemented when the device is used in landscape mode and the screen width is between 400 and 700 pixels.

CSS Media Queries[52] inspired by his idea, I created my own CSS media query module[53]for 40 different parameters. I performed the first test from a desktop

Fig.), with a (portrait) screen.

The figures below illustrate the test result; lines marked in green mean that the rule formulated in the given line is true for the given device.

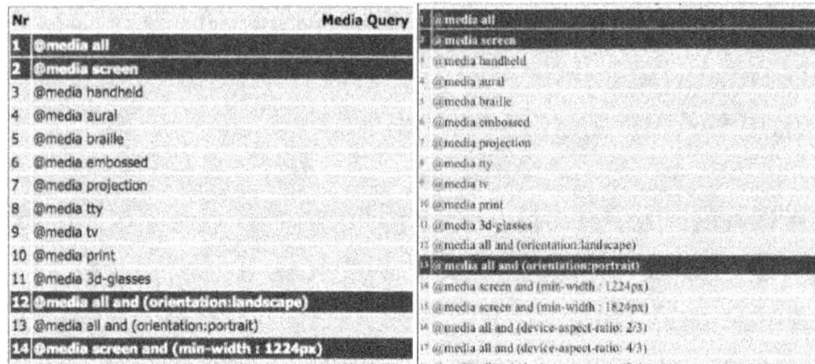

Nr	Media Query
1	@media all
2	@media screen
3	@media handheld
4	@media aural
5	@media braille
6	@media embossed
7	@media projection
8	@media tty
9	@media tv
10	@media print
11	@media 3d-glasses
12	@media all and (orientation:landscape)
13	@media all and (orientation:portrait)
14	@media screen and (min-width : 1224px)

1	@media all
2	@media screen
3	@media handheld
4	@media aural
5	@media braille
6	@media embossed
7	@media projection
8	@media tty
9	@media tv
10	@media print
11	@media 3d-glasses
12	@media all and (orientation:landscape)
13	@media all and (orientation:portrait)
14	@media screen and (min-width : 1224px)
15	@media screen and (min-width : 1824px)
16	@media all and (device-aspect-ratio: 2/3)
17	@media all and (device-aspect-ratio: 4/3)

Figure: iPhone device CSS media query

fortunately, the screenshot is not able to return the entire list, in any case, it can be seen that both the desktop computer and the smartphone can handle the all and screen properties. The computer has a landscape monitor (orientation:landscape), while the mobile device viewed the given page with a portrait display (orientation:portrait). In addition, the desktop computer is capable of up to 1224 pixels wide resolution, which is not characteristic of the phone.

The above property list can be expanded as desired, in a production environment the system obviously does not display the results of the queries for the user, it only uses them for the responsive design of the interface.

Just like for implicit data collection. Because the information collected in this way can travel from the client to the server every second thanks to the AJAX technology, where it is stored and readily used as input data for our recommender system.

A new, previously unused data collection technique in our system is the use of CSS media queries.

PROCESSING THE RESULT OF A CSS MEDIA QUERY

The basic idea is to scan the table containing the media properties and grab the rows that were recolored during detection. The rows of our table have a light brown background

CSS

As a result of the detection, we now have tangible data at our disposal, which we can easily send to our application server in the previously described JSON format.

DATA PROTECTION WITH AN EXPERT EYE

Computers store a lot of data about the user, both on the client and server side. One click, one second on a website and the owner of the web portal has recorded hundreds of different facts about the visitor. For this, you don't even need to equip the site with intelligent sensors, you just need to use web traffic analysis systems such as Google Analytics.

Whatever the method, let us have no illusions; everyday data collection is part of our Internet life.

This is fine as long as our data does not fall into unauthorized hands. Although we saw in the previous chapter the methods and types of data that web portals can collect about us, we need to worry less about the data stored on servers. On the one hand, they are physically well protected, and on the other hand, web service providers are subject to strict domestic and international regulations regarding data management.

On the client side, however, it is our responsibility to physically protect our computer and the sensitive data stored on it. The biggest problem is that most users are not even aware of the risks they are exposed to; in fact, you don't even know what data your own computer stores about you.

The research result below was inspired by my own expert research work, which I then supplemented with other experiences in the profession. In the next chapter, I would like to show how the data stored on the client side can be extracted and what information can be determined from them.

THEORETICAL BACKGROUND

Nowadays, there are many browsers to choose from, which differ in their appearance, services or even speed. From an expert point of view, however, they have one feature in common: their general technological feature is that before displaying a website, it

it is first downloaded from the web server and then displayed in the browser of the local computer. In order to be able to display the same website faster the next time, web browsers keep this downloaded data, so it remains available on the computer even after the user has already closed the browser or turned off the computer. Web files downloaded from this are called cache, history or temporary internet files; depending on the operating system and browser we use, these files are stored in different places on our computer.

Starting with Windows Vista, Windows 7 and 8 operating systemssystems, the temporary internet files stored by the Internet Explorer browser can be found in the following folder:

where <windowsUsername> is the current user's Windows login name. You can also find the browsing history, i.e. the URLs of previously visited websites, nearby:

There is an index.dat file in this folder, which is very useful if the user has already deleted his browsing history; the deleted history can be recovered by processing the file.

Mozilla Firefox stores browsing history in a database table in SQLite format, called the

can be reached via access route.

When Firefox is started for the first time, it automatically creates the profile folder, which contains the browsing history (places.sqlite), the list of downloaded files (download.sqlite) and the passwords stored by the browser (key3.db and *signons.sqlite*) containing files. Although these are not plain text files, they can be easily viewed by anyone using free software such as SQLite Database Browser.

Google Chrome also stores the history, downloaded files, and user names and passwords entered on websites:

Although the files here do not have the .sqlite extension, after examining the header part of the files, we found that they are actually files in SQLite format.

FINDING THE CLUES

We could go into more detail, because the list is not yet complete, but due to space limitations, we have limited ourselves to these. We prefer to discuss the available software tools that provide the opportunity to extract the above-mentioned data in a structured and automated manner.

BROWSING HISTORY MAPPING

We don't need to manually rummage through the temporarily stored files of a computer, there are many great applications for reconstructing our web browser activity.

What we do in Internet Explorer is the free IECacheView[54] or Internet Evidence Finder for business purposes[55] can be restored using Of course, ChromeCacheView exists for the same purpose[56]and ChromeHistoryView[57]for the Google Chrome browser and MozillaCacheView[58] and MozillaHistoryView[59]to extract data from Firefox browsers.

sing the software, we get a list that can be exported to different formats (pdf, xls, html) about when, what page and how many times we visited, and we can even find out

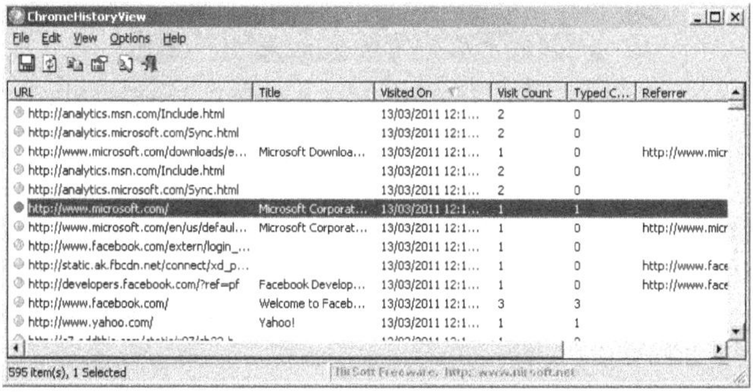

URL	Title	Visited On	Visit Count	Typed C...	Referrer
http://analytics.msn.com/Include.html		13/03/2011 12:1...	2	0	
http://analytics.microsoft.com/Sync.html		13/03/2011 12:1...	2	0	
http://www.microsoft.com/downloads/e...	Microsoft Downloa...	13/03/2011 12:1...	1	0	http://www.micr
http://analytics.msn.com/Include.html		13/03/2011 12:1...	2	0	
http://analytics.microsoft.com/Sync.html		13/03/2011 12:1...	2	0	
http://www.microsoft.com/	Microsoft Corporat...	13/03/2011 12:1...	1	1	
http://www.microsoft.com/en/us/defaul...	Microsoft Corporat...	13/03/2011 12:1...	1	0	http://www.micr
http://www.facebook.com/extern/login_...		13/03/2011 12:1...	1	0	
http://static.ak.fbcdn.net/connect/xd_p...		13/03/2011 12:1...	1	0	http://www.face
http://developers.facebook.com/?ref=pf	Facebook Develop...	13/03/2011 12:1...	1	0	http://www.face
http://www.facebook.com/	Welcome to Faceb...	13/03/2011 12:1...	3	3	
http://www.yahoo.com/	Yahoo!	13/03/2011 12:1...	1	1	

595 item(s), 1 Selected

which was the previous web page (referrer) from which we migrated to the current page.

EXTRACTING PASSWORDS

Even more interesting and critical information, there are also free solutions for mapping stored usernames and passwords. The IEPassView[60]PasswordFox[61]and ChromePass[62]software names speak for themselves, and the information they provide is quite impressive. We can find out which website was accessed with which username and password from the given computer (32. figure).

he biggest advantage of the free applications listed above is that they do not require any installation procedure, any of them can be run from a simple pen drive. If you think about it, these are very dangerous weapons in the hands of a cybercriminal. It is enough to leave our computer unattended for 2 minutes and all our confidential data has already been obtained.

PROTECTIVE MEASURES

As we saw in the previous chapter, there are many places on our computer where footprints of our Internet activity appear; there are many tools that can easily extract this data. The research results encourage the formulation of three simple methods in order to make it more difficult for our sensitive data to be leaked.

PASSWORD PROTECTION

The first and most important step is related to our passwords. We know very well that it is not a good idea to store our passwords written on a piece of paper stuck to the corner of a monitor, but we have seen that we are not safe even if our computer stores this information itself. Therefore, the most important advice beyond not letting strangers near your computer; do not ask or allow our browser to store login information.

On the other hand, if we are careful enough and identify ourselves with different passwords on each website, after a while we will be unable to remember them. Fortunately, all operating systems offer effective software solutions to keep our data safe; it is enough to remember a single master password, which then opens and makes visible the sensitive information stored behind it.

There is no point in storing our passwords in the world's most secure safe if those passwords can be easily guessed. An entire generation has grown up since the

Internet became an active part of our lives, yet to this day we still come across passwords that bear the name or date of birth of the owner's pet or family member.

Today, fortunately, most web systems require the entry of a password with the appropriate security level, such as uppercase and lowercase letters, numbers, and a minimum length of 8 characters.

THOUGHTFUL SOCIAL SHARES

As a second piece of advice, let's accept the fact that anything we share on a social network, upload to a website or send over Skype is out of our control. From that moment on, it is no longer our own data, it can appear anywhere, at any time.

Of course, we can trust that the picture sent to our friend will not get out of his hands, or that only our friends can see our pictures on Facebook, let's not fool ourselves; once you've shared anything with someone, it's potentially available to anyone.

It may be that our friend is not abusing our confidential information, but if he does not properly protect his data, our sensitive data is also at risk along with his own.

That is why we should pay special attention to sharing only data with anyone during our social life that will not pose a problem later if it becomes public.

It is an interesting fact and important to keep in mind that our Facebook profile can be a decisive argument for or against our application in a future job interview. Almost half of the managers and HR specialists said that a prospective employee's online life or Facebook profile influences their decision, while almost 30 percent of them think that the company has the right to fire an employee who communicates in an inappropriate style on their Facebook page [91].

After that, we really should think twice about what we write, what we say or what we share on social media, because it can affect our current or future work, our entire future existence.

THE CLEAN SHEET

The third and final conclusion: always keep in mind that every step we take on the Web leaves many footprints on our computer. That's why don't forget to regularly delete your browsing history, temporarily stored Internet files, conversations in Skype or other Messenger programs. Browser and communication programs provide this opportunity, deleting the browsing history is just two clicks and five seconds; take your time, it's really worth it.

SUMMARY

In my dissertation, I summarized the research work of the last 5 years, during which I tried to analyze in as much detail as possible the international results achieved so far in connection with intelligent web systems, to search for and recognize the areas where interesting challenges arise both from a scientific and professional point of view, and useful results can be obtained.

During my research work, I reworked the development process of web systems, and then offered a design pattern based on MVC principles that meets today's needs, which can also be used to integrate client-server frameworks. The appropriate display of the output data of intelligent web systems is crucial from the point of view of user experience and - not least - market profit, so on the one hand I proposed a new model for making existing and new web portals faster, and on the other hand I developed a new, AJAX-based implicit data collection method, which can be used to make the collection of information. Responsiveness and intelligence of the user interface are also of particular importance, so I proposed a universal, responsive, content-dependent system model that can be used for web systems with any theme.

The undisclosed purpose of my dissertation is to bring academic research closer together with the technologies used in industry and business life. Actors in scientific life are often accused of saying that most of their research results are of purely theoretical importance, are far from reality, and can be used in industry with difficulty or only after years. In this regard, IT is a particularly sensitive area, where both hardware and software technology change and develop extremely quickly.

During the past years, I was in the fortunate position that my work as a college instructor and active software and web developer contributed to a more detailed analysis and illumination of a topic just as much as the experiences gained during my duties as a forensic expert or CCNA instructor.

I tried to scrutinize the latest, current problems taken from business life and offer them a solution that uses and applies scientific results; at the same time, in addition to the theoretical results, it also offers practical, immediately usable and deployable methods.

Overall, the question I was looking for an answer to was: How can we make today's intelligent web systems better?

In this dissertation I summarized my research work of the past five years, when I focused on the detailed analyzes of the international results in intelligent web systems, in order to locate and identify areas, where interesting challenges and results may appear both in scientific and professional way.

In my research, I revised the development process of web systems, offered an MVC based software development design pattern that fits in nowadays modern methodologies and also suitable for client-server framework integration. Proper display of output data of intelligent web systems is a key regarding the aspect of user experience and market profit, so at first, I proposed a new model for existing and new web portals to make them faster and on the other hand, I developed a new AJAX-based implicit data collection method that improves information collection process more effectively. The intelligence and responsive behavior of a user interface has also considerable importance, thus I have created a universal, responsive, content-aware system, which is suitable for any themed web systems and finally I searched, systematized and presented the risk of web systems; where and how data is collected, stored about us, about the users.

As an unconcealed goal, my dissertation aims to bring closer to each other the academic research area and the technologies used in industry and business life. Academic researchers are often accused of the fact that most of their research results are purely theoretical, far from reality or just takes years to be utilized for the industry. From this point of view, information technology, which changes rapidly, is a particularly sensitive area, as well as hardware and software technology.

I tried to address the latest, current problems of real industrial and business life, find solutions that use and apply the scientific results; besides the theoretical results, I offer practical, immediately usable and deployable methods as well.

To sum it up, the question that needs to be answered is: How can we make nowadays used intelligent web systems better?

NEW RESULTS

The dissertation consists of six chapters which are closely related to each other where I overview the whole process of a web-based system. In the short reviews of the chapters I describe the initial problem and give my new research results and methods for the discussed problem.

It is just happened that I got insight into the scientific world as a young researcher, therefore it is my pleasure, that foreign researchers cite and use my results and my articles, so please allow me to mention the citations where it is relevant.

In the first chapter I reviewed the development process of web-systems, detected the shortcomings of currently used models and developed a new method that meets the demands of today's need.

The second chapter highlights the system design from the entire development process, describes in detail the traditional and trendy design patterns used today and then I worked out a new, MVC-based design pattern that is also suitable for the client-server framework integration as well .

The third chapter describes the performance shortcomings of current market leader web systems, reviews existing speed increasing technologies and offers a new process model that can be used to build fast web systems or improve existing web portal speed performance.

*Chapter four*presents an interesting, AJAX-based implicit data acquisition technology, which can make data collection very effective, serves the needs of responsive presentation and offers ideal data collection possibility for the recommender systems.

The fifth chapter is intended to be used in making better the component of the software system directly in contact with the user. The user interface developed by the improvements of the new model adapts intelligently for its display device, for its type and its screen resolution.

Finally, in the last, sixth chapter I explore, analyze and present the privacy risks of existing intelligent systems, I point out what risks are faced in our personal data in the Web 2.0 era.

ADAPTIVE DEVELOPMENT METHOD PROBLEM

The software development process is complicated and complex. Certain parts of it and the relationships between them require modeling in order to make the process modular and easily understandable. The most known and widespread model is the waterfall model. This model is excellent in cases when we know all the system requirements at the very beginning of the development process.

Unfortunately, in real life, customers cannot define exactly what they want at the beginning of the project; requirements change and refine during the development process. That is why the waterfall model is declined in many cases during business web development. The waterfall model is not prepared for this kind of changes; when a development phase has been completed, it is almost impossible to make any changes on it.

SOLUTION

We need a method, which is quite flexible and makes it possible to modify the design and system development process and architecture based on continuous customer consultations. Such a method is agile software development, although it cannot be used in many cases. Based on my research-development work, I combined both systems and created a new development model fitting today's modern web development process model, this is the adaptive development method.

INTEGRATED DESIGN PATTERN

PROBLEM

Nowadays it is impossible to develop web applications

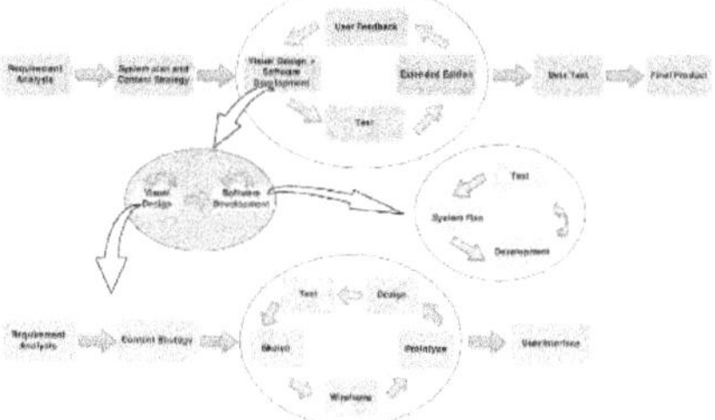

without proper design patterns, as developers must

serve both rich client-side programming tasks, as well as usual server-side engineering and coding. Whether the client side or server-side programming we are talking about, the volume of the work requires the use of design patterns. It is cumulatively true for a complex application, where client and server side development is in a necessarily indivisible relationship. The most popular design pattern is MVC. In this phase of my research I am searching for the answer whether this pattern is still suitable for nowadays development environments, whether it is possible to offer to the developers a new, better architecture integrating client and server side systems.

SOLUTION

After examination of different design patterns I concluded that the original MVC architecture, or more precisely, its modified, Cocoa version is the perfect initial state for developing a new integrated design pattern. Furthermore, my choice is verified by the fact that MVC frameworks are the most popular

development environments, both on the client and the server side.

Thus the real question is, how we can connect a JavaScript MVC with a PHP MVC framework in such a way that the new, integrated system also fits into the Model-View-Controller architecture.

Approaching from the server side, it is obvious that a View component needs further segmentation, as View complexity makes the development work harder. If we change the View component to a whole client-side MVC,

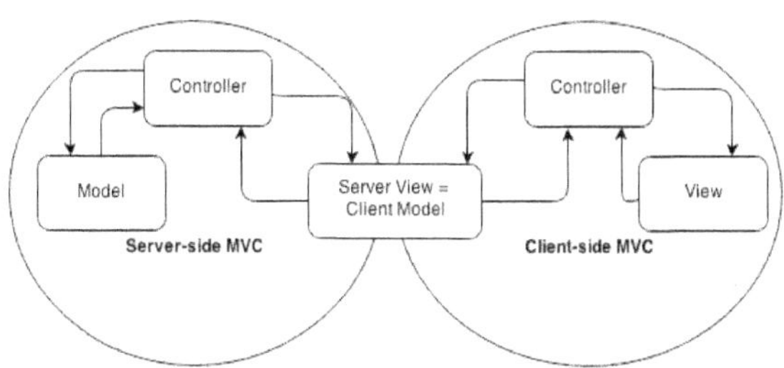

our new system be-comes an M(MVC)C.

In the case of client-side MVC, the Model component of an MVC pattern is a simple HTML code, and the View is a CSS file, (one CSS file means one View), whereas the Controller is the browser itself that assigns HTML with CSS. From another approach, View is a user interface born from a combination of HTML, CSS and data. JavaScript classes and methods play the role of a Controller, and the Model is the data coming from the web server.

Whichever aspect we take, the Model is the interface where a server-side MVC system could be attached. Based on this result, the following figure describes the new design pattern.

Fig. 2: Integrated Design Pattern

The developed new pattern was presented on SOFA2014 International Conference and my 14 pages article Integrated Design Pattern for Intelligent Web Applications was also accepted to appear.

MODEL FOR FASTER WEB SYSTEM PERFORMANCE

PROBLEM

As it is mentioned in the introduction, several researches confirm: a web system, based on an intelligent, excellent mathematical model, is worth nothing if the user can hardly wait for displaying the content. Clear proof of the importance of speed is that from 2010 Google has also begun to use webpage speed as an evaluation parameter in its PageRank algorithm. Several interesting books and scientific papers were published about making web pages faster, even the two biggest search engines, Google and Yahoo have also presented recommendations and measurement methods in this issue. However, based on surveys there are only a few web pages in the world that fully meet the proposed technical guidelines. Examining the top 10 visited webpages of the world,

SOLUTION

In the third phase of my research I tested and applied methods proposed by literature and my own experiences on a 4000 unique visitors a day web portal. Based on the results of performance analysis I created a method collection that is suitable not only for converting existing web pages, but can also be applied in the design phase, thus greatly facilitating the births of faster intelligent web systems.

With the title Improved Speed on Intelligent Web Sites I published my related results in 2013, which aroused the attention of Egyptian scientists, they cite my work in their XML Schema-Based Minification for

Communication of Security Information and Event Management (SIEM) Systems in Cloud Environments (DOI: 0.14569/IJACSA.2014.050912) paper published in International Journal of Advanced Computer Science and Applications.

IMPLICIT DATA COLLECTION, A NEW MODEL PROBLEM

Using recommender systems is the main tool for implementing personalized web content. However, most of current research faces a problem that it is very hard to gather real data in adequate quantity and quality, so the majority of scientists work on sample databases or the so fortunate minority of them can apply their data and text mining methods on real systems.

But even in the case of highly frequented and well known web systems like amazon.com or eBay.com it is very difficult to convince users to constantly fill out surveys, provide preference values. First of all, it is a time-consuming task, on the other hand, users are wary, they tend to give out information about themselves less and less frequently.

SOLUTION

That is why related researches are moving towards implicit data collection. During implicit data collection, web-based systems can continuously collect and process large amounts of data in an unobtrusive way. In this part of my research I provide a new, AJAX-based technology to make data acquisition more efficient.

Although I published the results in my AJAX-Based Data Collection Method for Recommender Systems title article in 2012, the method described therein is still current, a trio of Korean researchers, Sung Moon Bae et al cited it in their Utilization of Demographic Analysis with IMDB User Ratings on the Recommendation of Movies (DOI: 10.7838/jsebs.2014.19.3.125) paper.

RESPONSIVE AND CONTENT-AWARE PRESENTATION

PROBLEM

Personalized web content is extremely important just as the fact that systems can be able to provide it in a user friendly way. The major drawback of earlier web systems is that they have not provided the so-called "application feeling" to the user, the method "we click and get the content immediately" which was familiar in desktop environment has not been prevailed due to the characteristics of a client-server architecture. The browser waits until it gets the answer for its request, so does the user as well. Each of us has spent several seconds in front of a computer waiting for web pages to load or refresh. Developers intended to remedy this deficiency with the asynchronous communication capabilities of AJAX.

In addition, thanks to mobile device penetration and due to the introduction of Ipv6 as we can connect the Internet from our refrigerator or coffee maker as well, developers have to face a new challenge: it is not enough to develop content-dependent web systems, device-dependent web pages will own the future.

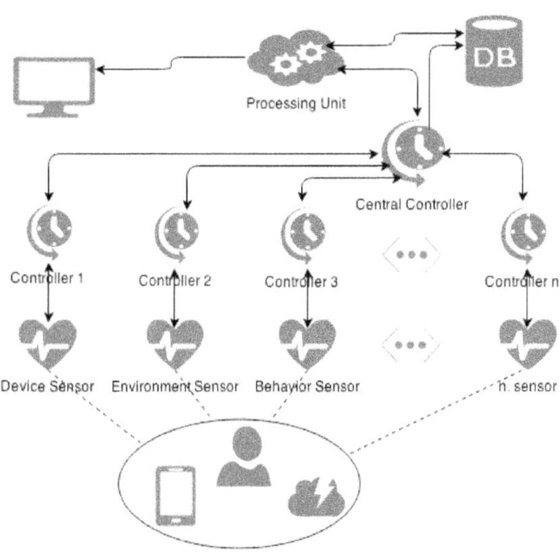

SOLUTION

Accordingly, user interfaces developed with the mentioned model adapt intelligently to the device that displays it, to its type and screen resolution. The information acquired about users is divided into three different groups: Device, Environment and Behaviour. These categories are carried on the data collection based on the following sensor architecture.

Fig. 3: Sensor architecture

Based on the information collected, the application server assembles the most appropriate content for the user, creates the user interface and sends it to the client device.

PRIVACY FROM A FORENSIC POINT OF VIEW

PROBLEM

Right to privacy issues constantly arise related to intelligent web systems, because information security and personal data protection are key issues today. The invisible and continuous data collection has paramount importance not only of intelligent systems, but in terms of our entire life spent on the Internet.

As a forensic expert I worked in several criminal cases, where I had to discover the footprints of Internet usage on a given computer.

SOLUTION

Experiences are surprising and enlightening. I had the pleasure to examine several aspects of the issue; so the point of view of the user, of the expert, of the criminal or of the investigating authority. The last phase of my research is focused on finding out the kind of information that has been collected and stored about a user by web-based systems, how and by what kind of tools, methods is it possible to identify and to defend against unauthorized hands .

I wrote two papers about results in this area in 2012. The first one was Using Forensic Techniques for Internet Activity Reconstruction, which was cited by Chinese researchers, Chen Long and others cited it in their User browsing-data recovery of Google browser in private-browsing mode (DOI: 0.3979/j.issn.1673-

825X.2013.06.027) article, while the second one, Social media risks from forensic point of view was useful for Mohammad Reza Keyvanpour and his Iranian researcher colleagues in 2014. They cited it in their Digital Forensics 2.0 (DOI: 10.1007/978-3-319-05885-6_2) paper. It is a special pleasure that the latter article is mentioned by the web page of Information Systems Information Analysis Center (CSIAC) supported by the American Department of Defense.

www.ingramcontent.com/pod-product-compliance
Lightning Source LLC
LaVergne TN
LVHW012109160826
845678LV00014B/3009

9798353397564